Symbols of Power
In Metaphysics

Life on the Other Side of the Veil

The Edge of Passage Series
Book Two

Mathias Karayan

Mathias Karayan

www.karayanpublishing.com
Or you can contact:
matt@karayanpublishing.com

Library of Congress Control Number
2011900517

Editing: Jackie Jeffery

Proof: Rita Ann

Drawings by Maria Monterey

ISBN-13: 978-1545405444

Books by Mathias Karayan
*
The Edge of Passage Series

To start your journey involves the conviction that *there is more to living than what your world offers.* The desire to want to step beyond this view is to start your journey home. As you begin to recognize your time as a passing through, being a passerby, you begin to understand the messages of what people and events are really about. This is what *The Edge of Passage Series* is about. Wherever you go you take yourself with you. Are you ready?

The first book in the series, **The Way Home: Stories from the Master,** deals with the paradoxical experience of living life on life's terms. To transcend the paradox is an experience in non-dualistic thinking.

The second book in the series, **Symbols of Power in Metaphysics: Life on the Other Side of the Veil,** addresses the experience of brushing up against the veil; life from the other side. Psychic experiences, astral-projection, past life memories, reincarnation and karma are among the topics discussed. Most of us have had these experiences but have dismissed them as a fanciful dream or just strange. This book explores the language of and blocks to experiencing life on the other side of the veil.

Symbols of Power in Philosophy: What the great minds of our past have to teach us about today's issues, is the third book in the series. This book deals with the issues of what the great minds of our past dealt with. Are we evolving or are we spinning our wheels in the mud? There is a common thread among our teachers of days gone by about today's issues..

Transformational Psychotherapy: Theory and Practice, is the fourth book in *The Edge of Passage Series.* This book for the 21st century, addresses what Transformational Psychotherapy is, how it is applied to topics of conversation in psychology and how healing occurs.

The fifth book, **Reflections for the Wandering Mind: A Book on Meditation,** is about a unified goal for peace of mind. This book is not about changing your world so you can have peace. Peace is not there! This book is about correction at the level of your mind. It is the experience of your miracle when your mind transcends its conflicted thinking. This book contains lessons that allow your mind to experience the peace that awaits your remembrance.

Words of Love: A book on Healing Relationships, is the sixth book in the series which asks, "What is love and how is it to be found?" This book is about your journey to experience love, and the healing of relationships that struggle with a lack of love. It is about the removal of your blocks to love's awareness. *Words of Love* illuminates your journey to love's experience.

The seventh book; ***In the Light of Passage: Three Short Stories on Life's Journey,*** are stories; of a man lost in the forest, trying to find his way home with the help of some strange new friends. An overworked counselor is sent on an unexpected quest of self-discovery. A climber seeks adventure on an infamously dangerous mountain steeped in supernatural stories. With these characters' journeys, *In the Light of Passage* explores the lessons we learn in life and what it means to live.

Book eight, ***Awakening to the Christ Within: What Jesus really taught,*** takes a scholarly look at the text of the Bible as a means to experience what Jesus was really about. It is a full circle return to the first book, to the message of the Master, as to how to walk in the world yet not be of the world.

Also by Mathias Karayan
*

Healing the Wound

The Family's Journey through Chemical Dependency

All writings of truth are not the Truth
They are about the Truth
We just give them meaning
Which makes them
Symbols of Power [1]

---

[1] All beliefs, disciplines of learning, psychology, sociology, philosophy, theology, Ideologies, politics, economics, ecology and education, etc., are built on and sustained by the meanings you have given them. When you withdraw the meaning you have given any symbol, the symbol dies. Society is *a collective hunch; a* conditioned thinking built upon layers of meanings, symbols of power made sacred over time.

Mathias Karayan

Acknowledgment

Thank you Jackie Jeffery for your dedication to keeping this material internally consistent.

Thank you Cory Yenor, who, when I would doubt myself, encouraged me to write on.

To my friends in Spirit; Michael Weinauer, Annalicia Niemela, Maria Monterey and Kate Evans.

Dedication

To Rita,
My intuitive sweetheart
You remind me that the whirlwind ...
... is just a dance

Prologue to the Second Edition

The topics in this book have not been the result of an intellectual study. When I first wrote this book, I was not well read on the subject of metaphysics. In fact, I had not read anything at all on the subject. Nor did I believe any of it. I was a true skeptic.[2] However, because of my direct experience with *the other side of the veil,* I was compelled to put into words that which is beyond words. My direct experiences in the section "Beyond the Veil"[3] in the back of this book are the basis for these writings.

Mathias Karayan
February 2018

---

[2] Skepticism in philosophy is the doctrine that denies the possibility of attaining knowledge of reality as it is in itself, apart from human perception. *Symbols of Power in Philosophy p13*
[3] *Beyond the Veil p195-207*

Those who think they live in space and time, relate to and communicate through the symbols of space and time.

It is through the intention of love that I write about the experience of the other side ... using the symbols of space and time.

Matt Karayan
2011

Mathias Karayan

TABLE OF CONTENTS

Section I
Symbols of Power and Life's Continuity

Introduction 14
1) What is Metaphysics? 19
2) Teachers of Healing 20
3) What Healing Is and How It Is Accomplished . 23
4) Beyond the Senses 33
   The Senseless Mind 47
5) The Earth: Your Reflection 48
6) The Concept of Magic 60
7) Cultures of Lore 67
8) Dreaming Realms of Consciousness 72
   The Art of Dream Interpretation 73
   Realms of Consciousness 81
   Experiences from Beyond the Dream 88
   Another Dream State 93
   The Time of In-Between 96
9) Karma 98
   Karma and Your Destiny 99
   Where is Karma? 109
   The Lash of the Dragon's Tail 110
10) Life's Continuity 119
   Clarifying the Relationship between
     Reincarnation, Karma & Recollection . . 120
   Any Body Will Do 133
   Nothing's Way 144
   Déjà Vu 145

Section II
Symbols of Power and Your Creative Self

1) Your Creative Self 147
   Healing as an Expression of Your
      Creative Self 148
   Self-Deception: The Primary Block to
      Expressing Your Creative Self 162
   Communicating from Your Creative Self . . . 170
2) Spiritual Guides 181
   I Send You 182
3) Song & Dance 184
4) Reflections 186
   The King of In-Between 187
   Elements 189
   No Man's Land 190
   Courage 191
   In The Arms of God 192
   I Am You 194
5) Beyond the Veil 195
   Vision Quest 197
   Once Before 198
   All Are Called 200
   The Desert of Colorless Dreams 201
   The Power of the Void 202
   Merging with the Light 203
   Beyond the Horizon of Light 205
   I Met Him 206
   Wake Up! 207
Appendix
   Women of The Moon 208
Glossary 252

Introduction

This book is based on the premise that whatever is temporal in nature cannot be taken seriously as true or real ... but it can be used as metaphors of release towards the healing of your mind.

Religion in all its forms is the expression of one's search to reunite with Spirit. The body, properly perceived can be used as a means for healing; a tool to once again hear Spirit's call. Likewise, all psychic, supernatural, out of body and miraculous experiences are expressions of a consciousness beyond the body's senses. Though they are temporary in nature, they can be used as aids to break through your beliefs about a world untrue ... to remember Spirit's call.

I am not talking about a time or place you have not been to. I am talking about an experience you already know beyond the beliefs you use to block your memory of that experience. **All beliefs about ever-changing forms are symbols of power that limit your mind to a temporary experience.** *This is the definition of all sickness.* Because of your investment in these symbols of limitation, you must use them as your means to free your mind from them ... to remember your Eternal Self.

This book is for those who consciously practice *facilitating* healing for themselves and for others. It contains clarifications of some symbols of "the new age" that have been misinterpreted to enslave your mind to limits of experience. Because all symbols of the world represent forms that are temporary in nature, the teaching principles in this book can be generalized to *all disciplines* of thought.

The curriculum presented in this book is in direct opposition to the world's curriculum. The world teaches you to be a better judge for decision. This curriculum teaches that to relinquish judgment is your journey to freedom, for it is your beliefs about a world untrue that has enslaved you.[4]

To judge is to invite conflict. To relinquish judgment is to allow peace of mind to be itself.

The world's judgments are substitutions, distractions, mediating forms of beliefs that limit you to the experience of a duality of thought;[5] thoughts that bring your mind into conflict with itself and thus fear. This book is an approach to help you relinquish judgment; to remember your creative Self with Source, should you so choose.

The power of any symbol is established by belief.
When you withdraw value from that belief,
The symbol dies.

Your miracle is the changing of your mind about any symbol of belief as you withdraw value from it. It is the changing of *how* you perceive *what* you perceive. It is addressing the problem where it was made ... in your mind. And this you can change.

---

[4] For those who say, "You have to have judgments to survive or to operate in the world," are those who believe their judgments protect them. This book suggests that your judgments are the cause of your fears!
[5] *Symbols of Power in Philosophy p35-49*

Checkmate

And now I look out from my mountain
And see the soldiers in the field
It won't be long now 'til they have me
This time advance guards are for real

Come on, come on
Take me there, take me there
I don't care where we go
Take me, I just want to know what I used to
know

James Seals
Advance Guards

Section I

Symbols of Power
And
Life's Continuity

The beginning is the place you've already been.

Moving forward is the illusion of wanting to get to the end ... yet it is but to remember the beginning.

Today is but a ripple of that place in time.

What Is Metaphysics?

Real forgiveness as the only function meaningful in time is your solution to your spiritual dilemma. Any conversation regarding the metaphysical without real forgiveness, is meaningless banter.

Metaphysics is a traditional branch of philosophy relating to the transcendent; an experience other than what is perceptible through the body's senses.

This book defines sickness as separation; separation from a Greater Self that your identity is defined by. This dis-relation from Self is projected as the conflict of dualistic thinking, represented as the Eternal Self vs a temporal make believe self, an inner world vs an external make believe world. From this comes all your conflicting goals, projected as a world seemingly outside of your perceiving mind. Your sickness is played out by the giving of your mind over to symbols, beliefs, ideologies, that limit your experience to sensation and perception of an outer world. Although you are not the product of the symbols of form that nature vs nurture present to your mind, your mind does play out your sickness or spiritual dilemma of dis-relation through the guise of nature, nurture, and social conditioning.

There is another experience other than your outer world. This is what metaphysics is about.

Mathias Karayan

Teachers of Healing

This book is for the healer; the healed healer; the one who understands what part real forgiveness plays in your journey towards waking up. That is why;

The healed healer stands as a light
Beyond the dream.

Introduction

Teachers of healing, because **all beliefs about ever-changing forms are symbols of power that limit your mind to a temporary experience,** you are not asked to go beyond all symbols the world offers, for you still have work to do. For a while, as a teacher, you need to use the symbols the world uses for meaning so you can communicate with those you meet along your way. But do not be deceived by them for they do not represent anything. For the experience of One Mind cannot be found in them.

Your Need

Teacher, if you teach another to see that *they experience what they first think*, you both can heal. If you allow for no exceptions to this principle, you will come to understand that *you are the cause* of the world you experience. In other words, sickness did not choose you, you chose sickness. A sick mind is not open-minded on this point. However, if you chose sickness, you can choose again! You will heal as you remember to teach that; *No symbol has power over you except the power you gave it, and this you can change.*

When you recognize that you interpret the world through what you first believe, you come to realize that your need is not to forgive the other person for what they did to you. Your need is to forgive yourself for how you decided to interpret *what you thought* another did to you.[6] Not only will you recognize the power your mind has to deceive itself, but you will also recognize the power your mind has to free itself from the reoccurring disturbances presented as lessons in different forms. These forms are the same lesson waiting for you to forgive your perception of what never was. To every disturbance you perceive, say to yourself as a mantra;[7]

I am deceived by nothing in a form I desire.[8]

Teachers, you have a commission to fulfill. Be diligent to understand what meanings you give to the forms you choose. Let no form be a deception to delay release for your mind or you will teach delay to others.

Waking up

Healers, you may have spiritual revelations, psychic experiences, glimpses of enlightenment. You are waking from a long deep slumber, slowly shaking off the depths of despair, a drunken withdrawal, a feverish nightmare, the last frost of winter. Slowly you are being gently nudged into a peaceful calm, a restful sleep ... eventually to

---

[6] This is the principle of real forgiveness.
[7] A phrase repeated to aid concentration.
[8] A Course In Miracles

awaken into the arms of Love with a joyous realization that you never left.

Enlightenment is not an evolving into. It is not change. It is a recognition. Be not deceived by the ego's definition of enlightenment. To wake up is to be free of all judgment and guilt. It is the undoing of your karma.

Summary

Be patient with yourself.[9] Be patient with others. They come to teach you an ancient lesson forgotten through eons of time. Your journey through is not a regurgitating of what you thought another did to you. *Your need is to undo, forgive yourself for how you decided to interpret what you thought another did to you.* Teach this to others so you can learn it. You do not journey alone to your awakening. You journey back to You, the experience of One Mind, the Mind we all share. In the meantime,

Because denial is massive
Repetition becomes your best teacher.[10]

---

[9] *The Way Home p100*
[10] *The Way Home p171*

What Healing Is and How It Is Accomplished

Healer, because the body dies,
"Heal thyself" means what?

Introduction

No one heals anyone but themselves. Healer, what a strange situation you find yourself in. Your work is to facilitate healing for someone who perceives them-self as sick, so *you* can wake up!

Three Points for Reflection

Before you can facilitate healing with someone who perceives themselves as sick, three points to reflect on are important for consideration.

The understanding that:
1) No symbol (belief) has power over you except the power you give it.

And the questions of clarification that ask,
2) What are the symbols of power (beliefs) you employ in your life?

All beliefs, judgments, substitutions and mediating forms are symbols of power you hold dear when you use them to explain your world. And those symbols limit the power of your mind to the world of the ever-changing when they are used by you to try to understand and explain a world untrue to what you are in truth.

3) Do these symbols enslave you or do they free you?

Everything you think in your world symbolizes a belief that limits how you are to view people things and events. For example, the concept of evil is a symbol of power that can be used to frame a world view of judgment and fear. Or the belief in technology as your means for comfort and progress becomes a savior you can't live without. These are beliefs of magical thinking that distract you from where your journey lies. It lies within, not in a world of distraction, ideologies, symbols of beliefs that limit your mind to interpretations, to a world of judgment and fear. From this point of view, healing becomes the process of undoing by sorting out fact from fiction.

The honest consideration of these three points and the understanding of the next five principles make all the difference between being an unhealed healer or a healed healer.

Five Principles

When you have a problem, it will be obvious that:

1) The problem: In the world of trying to make the ever-changing meaningfully important, you have limited your mind to interpretations of opposition and absolutism. This you do to combat the doubt of a meaningless world.[11] Through your beliefs can you only experience what to believe within those chosen limits.[12] *This is the definition of sickness.* The symbols you use to communicate in your world is a presentation of confusing metaphors that reflects your internal conflict of separation. For

---

[11] All ideologies are made out of doubt to combat doubt.

[12] Selective perception.

example, how do you make compatible a loving God that sends part of His Creation to hell? Or given our so called great strides in technology and communication world wide, how do you account for humanity's inability to learn from the history of their past mistakes of war after war after war?[13] Only through fictitious, religious or magical thinking, at the cost of your mind's integrity[14] can this be done. Yet, only to be done to the mind that thinks it.

2) The cause of sickness: You are the cause of your sickness. You have given the power of your mind over to conflicting beliefs that demonstrate a world of separation experienced as real. And because you have empowered the meaningless as something important, you look out there for solutions, placebos, body issues, ideologies, games to occupy your time, to avoid looking at the cause of your sickness as within.

3) The clarification: Because the body dies, "Heal Thyself" cannot mean heal the body.[15] In the final analysis, sickness and health have nothing to do with a body. ***Healing is always about and for the mind.***

4) The goal: If separation is sickness, then *peace of mind* would be *a unifying goal* towards healing.[16]

---

[13] *Symbols of Power in Philosophy*
[14] The cost of your mind's integrity is to depreciate it's power by limiting it to beliefs or symbols of power.
[15] I do not deny that healings of the body seem to occur. But if your primary goal is to heal the body, in the end it will fail you and die. *The Way Home p162-165*
[16] *Reflection for the Wandering Mind p24-35*

5) The means to healing: Because you have empowered symbols to limit you to experience conflictual separation, you also have the power to change your mind about them through forgiveness. In fact, *any kind of healing is always the result of forgiveness.* This makes you your own means for healing as you commit to wanting a unified goal of peace with everyone you meet. Simply stated; *To heal is for you to release yourself from the limits you have imposed on your mind.*

Changing Your Mind

The power of any symbol is established by belief. When you withdraw value from that belief … the symbol dies.[17]

The means to peace as a unified goal are experiences that transcend your beliefs (symbols of power). This involves a change of mind about any particular belief that enslaves your view to a limited experience. Your expansive experiences are those you call epiphanies, miracles, "Oh I never thought about it that way" experiences. It is using your symbols of power once used to limit or separate, to heal your mind towards a unified goal for peace. Remember, *all beliefs about ever-changing forms are symbols of power that limit your mind to a temporary experience.*

For example, to take personal a person trying to hurt you through their behavior or words, involves a limiting belief. You know it is limiting because it brings conflict to your mind; conflict in the form of

[17] *The Way Home p149-151*

anger, guilt and fear, etc. That belief represents a symbol of power you used to limit you to an experience of feeling attacked. How can you receive healing with that belief in the way?

You do have choices should you want to withdraw value from that belief. In other words, to identify with the other person would be to see them like you. Like you, they also have times where they get caught up acting out their own life dilemma. I am not saying what anyone does or says is OK. I am saying that you empowered a limiting view to take it personally. The other person, not unlike you also takes things personally by acting out their confusion and ignorance by saying or doing what appears to be hurtful things. And without a reinterpretation or change of mind about that limiting view (symbol of power), you invited conflict into your mind. This is what the making of your karma is all about.

Aside from focusing on unacceptable behaviors that the other person needs to change, like "hers are worse than mine," your view of her is the result of conflict in your mind. And a mind in conflict is a mind in conflict with itself first. The hard part in this is your resistance to take responsibility for your part. Stop trying to justify your view as righteous so you can change your mind about it! Degrees of who's behavior is more acceptable or justifiable, become irrelevant. It is your mind you need to change for healing to occur, not anybody else's.

I tried to heal myself of my obsessed and ashamed mind with my obsessive and ashamed mind. You know how well that works.

Anne Lamott

A miracle is a change of mind, a withdrawal of value from a particular belief that has blocked you from your experience of peace of mind. *This is the only value any symbol has.*[18] To heal a sick mind with sick thinking is an impossible task. You seem to need redirection from outside of your mind to help you change direction.[19]

The Practitioner's Role

The exceptional teacher is one whose students say, "I have no need of you anymore."

To facilitate healing, the proper role of all practitioners is to help whoever you meet to re-frame all symbols (limiting beliefs) they present so they can eventually understand that healing comes from within. Healer, your client comes to you for a reason. Therefore, you become a mediating form and thus a symbol of power. Allow for no dependency to occur or you become just another idol for them.[20]

The Practitioner's Responsibility

Knowing is mind's natural disposition. All symbols that limit your mind, limit it from the experience of knowing. To not know is to experience doubt. In the light of doubt are beliefs made (symbols of power) to understand your world. However, they deny you the experience of knowing

---

[18] *The Way Home p62-64*
[19] The book *Reflections for the Wandering Mind* is all about; a redirection away from your circular thinking.
[20] The dynamics of a cult leader.

"You" directly. Your beliefs about a world not true is reinforced through selective perception. To selectively perceive is to see only what your beliefs want you to see to reinforce the experience of your beliefs as true.

You do not believe what you see.
You see what you want to believe.

Because your limiting beliefs block your experience of knowing directly, they reinforce the deception that you are something you are not. To not know, engenders fear and a search for meaning outside of knowing. And thus, in the world of doubt, belief and faith become needed to want to know. However, the solution is not to be found in the world of people, things and events. It is in the mind that made the world a place to not find your solution. This conflict of mind, projected away as a world of conflict is a breeding ground of anger, guilt and fear as seemingly real. If you are not aware of your projection, you will interpret the anger, guilt and fear that you put outside of you, as attack.

Given this dilemma, *it becomes the healer's responsibility to help their client re-interpret their perception of attack that seems to be coming from outside them-self, as an opportunity to heal.* The therapeutic form used is irrelevant when it is used as an opportunity to undo any idea of attack as real. The healed healer understands how to help their client reframe symbols that divide, as opportunities to heal. Pace yourself to work with where your client is at. Be patient. Remember to listen. You do not need to change them. This they do when they are ready.

How Healing is Accomplished

The task of the practitioner is to deny your client's denial of truth. This is not about confronting your client about what the truth is. It is about the practitioner's ability to look through their client's denial to identify with them on some level as sharing the same One Mind. It is a view that looks past any sickness your client presents. What you mistook as a problem in your client is your opportunity to see it as something different. You see the end game; a unified goal for peace of mind. With the end in view, the means to get there is always provided.[21] That is how healing is accomplished.

The unhealed healer is one who cannot see beyond their own misinterpretation as attack. They, like the client they are trying to help, are unknowingly enslaved by their own symbols of power. Teacher, facilitating opportunities for healing has only one requirement; humility.

Don't think you know the way.
For if you did you would not be here!

The Client's Role

When your client understands that it is in their best interest to see the problem as starting with them, the way they decided to see it, they will also see the opportunity to heal. When they can ask in all situations, "What is going on with me that I see this in a conflictual way?" they deal with the situation in the place it began. *Through the repetition of application,* your client learns that it is

---

[21] *Reflections for the Wandering Mind p32-33*

in their best interest to perceive all conflict as an opportunity to heal.[22] The door is open for healing to occur.

A particular problem does not mean the content or solution is different than any other form of sickness. Learning how to forgive this particular problem can be generalized to all problems your life seems to encounter. While different in form, they are all the same in content. The content is a mind that has enslaved itself to a limiting belief that looks different in form. Don't be fooled by the ever-changing forms of nothingness presented to a mind wanting to be deceived by nothingness.

Now the problem can be solved because your client sees the source of the problem as with the mind that saw it in that particular way. If your client chooses to hold on to interpretations that engender anger, guilt and fear, they are not ready to hear the call for healing. They will have to wait for the mediating form that does not threaten their chosen world view. Their readiness will allow for the next lesson in a form they can recognize and accept.

The Fear of Healing

The fear of healing which includes *the holding on to* anger, guilt, pain, pleasure and depression as justified, are beliefs your client holds dear. Your client holds these beliefs dear because their world view of how things "should" work, feels threatened.[23] For security sake, rules and boundaries are made to protect fixed beliefs /

---

[22] *The Way Home p104-107*

[23] This is what makes symbols sacred idols. Any symbol in need of protection is an idol because Truth needs no defense.

sacred symbols. Yet the more rules you have to secure safety, the more opportunity you have to have them broken. And when broken, either you or some unsuspecting soul should be punished for the violation.[24] There is no safety in this.

Your client's denial is the refusal to see that what they think will bring peace of mind is actually causing conflict. Your client's greatest need is the courage to understand that they do not really know what they think they know.[25] The facilitator of healing will be able to pace them self with the client's process of unfolding.

Healer, how often have you deceived yourself into making nothing mean something?[26] Your client can remind you of this when you see through their presenting problem for what it really is; a mis-thought needing correction. Don't forget, your clients are also your teachers. They come to you for healing. Let their experiences facilitate healing for you as well!

Summary

Your solution is always in the same place the problem was made; in the mind that thought it. It cannot be found anywhere else. A mind that is divided in its goal is a sick mind. The goal is *unified* when it is *only* peace of mind. A unified goal is how you and your client remove the blocks that keep you from remembering the experience of this peace.

---

[24] This is what a savior figure is all about.
[25] Your reaction to your perception of fear strengthens your belief that the fear is real. You can transform any experience of fear as a call for love. *The Way Home p53*
[26] The road is treacherous for those who do not know that they are lost to their own chosen road signs.

Beyond the Senses

Source is known to the mind, not the senses.
As long as the mind is led by the senses
You cannot know Source.

Introduction

Brain is a function of body.[27] Mind is a function used by Spirit for expression. Because your mind has blocked its natural disposition to know, it perceives. Mind interprets its perception of body sensations as either something to desire or something to avoid, pleasure and pain. Within the limits of the body's realm of pleasure and pain, is the experience of birth and death. This makes your investment in a body as an end in itself. When mind takes on a body as a self, the expression and memory of Spirit is blocked by the interference of the body's senses. Just below the conscious level, you are choosing continuously.

To *know* is to experience Self as Source's Creation. To *believe* is to experience something else; an individual body in a world of change. This is where your journey began. *Placing the body you think you are into proper perspective is paramount in understanding how to journey home.* Resistance is the ego's tactic of diversion. It is a maneuver signifying a desire not to know because its existence is at stake. Its last fierce defense for existence wants you to believe you are a body … right up to the body's death. You may resist what follows. Be open to another possibility.

---

[27] Mind and brain are two different things. The body's brain (physiology) belongs to the body. To study the brain as if it is mind is senseless confusion.

Mathias Karayan

A Moment of Thoughtlessness

*"A human being **falsely identifies himself** with his physical form because the life currents from the soul are breathed-conveyed into the flesh with such intense power that man **mistakes the effect for a cause,** and idolatrously imagines the body to have life of its own."[28]*

In an instant of thoughtlessness[29] mind entertained a thought separate from Source. Through this thought consciousness was made. Consciousness, viewing itself as separate[30] from Source, divided into a consciousness of many. The idea of a separation that could never be, was thoughtless mind's detour into confusion, self-deception and fear.[31] To protect itself from the fear of a separation that could never be, your mind in confusion defined its separateness as an identity, an ego made out of a collection of individually related thoughts.[32] Ego, in an attempt to survive,

---

[28] Paramahansa Yogananda from Autobiography of a Yogi, p472

[29] This instant of thoughtlessness seems a long time ago only because it has been buried under eons of beliefs with the hope of being forgotten.

[30] The beginning of dualistic thinking; I – You / subject - object.

[31] In terms of Christian theology this is the "original sin," the loss of innocence, the fall from the Garden of Eden. In existential psychology, this is the source of all "separation anxiety," the human dilemma of being in dis-relation with Self.

[32] *Transformational Psychotherapy p55-65,117-125*

searches for a place to reside to explain its experience of confusion and justify its fear as real.

Yeah we're playing those mind games forever
Projecting our images in space and in time

John Lennon
Mind Games

Through the power and projection of a confused mind, an ego identity of loosely related thoughts identifies with an earthen vessel[33] to hide behind. Surprised in the delight of this association with a body of sensation, your mind found gratification of pleasure. As your mind became drunk with dependence in this experience of pleasure, pain was never far behind. In an attempt to avoid pain, pleasure through the body became the goal. Because the only thing pleasure invites is pain, *your life becomes a preoccupation to achieve pleasurable experiences and avoid pain.*[34]

The body suffers as a distraction so your mind won't see how it has made itself victim to itself. Your body's suffering is a front to hide where the source of suffering comes from; your mind. Because of your dis-relation with Source, anger, grieving, guilt, frustration, fear and despair are always waiting just below this conscious level.

Not only does mind use a body to defend an individual consciousness of separation that would

---

[33] Ephemeral body; short-lived, fleeting, transitory.
[34] A basic tenet of Buddhism is that all living beings have the same basic wish to be happy and avoid suffering. Very few people understand the real causes of happiness and suffering.

be subject to physical pain, it also made a world of space, time, movement and noise to hide behind the thought of a separation that could never be. Thus, a world was made by an impossible thought, divided and subdivided as a collection of separate minds, unknown to Source. This impossible thought is the primary experience a mind lost in self-deception[35] vigorously defends as the only experience that is real.

Because truth needs no justification, a body is needed to defend your self-deception. Your biggest symbol of power is the body you seem to be.

Communication Lost

You sacrificed the experience of knowing as One Mind when you chose a thought separate from Source. You can choose again. However, your preoccupation with the body you think you are is the primary block you employ to prevent remembering your relationship of knowing. Because knowing was denied through the choices consciousness provides, doubt, belief and faith became the norm[36] as you entered into the nightmare of dualistic thinking.[37] Everything on earth is subject to differing points of view, interpretation and change. It is self-deception to attribute certainty to anything such as

---

[35] You think you are a separate individual because you seem to be a body. However, *hidden from your view* is the fact that you actually think you are a body because you first thought yourself to be separate. Individuality follows separation.

[36] All symbols of substitution from not knowing.

[37] *Symbols of Power in Philosophy p35-49*

religion, politics, morality, ethics, etc. All of this is played out as the making of human history.

How can the meeting of meaning occur when everything that is ever-changing continues to mean different things to each individual? When meaning is established by the accepting of shared symbols that egos can understand, you have an ego alliance of division and differences.[38] With the ego's defense of these shared differences as truth, nationalistic ideology and the clash of bodies (war) becomes justifiable. However, meaning need not be sacrificed. Meaning can be established and shared with another through any symbol of power that allows you both a shared experience of peace. This is the only value any symbol has.[39]

The Heart of Every Problem

It would be mistaken to give the impression that the five senses are worthless or bad. The senses are necessary for the body's functioning in a world of change. However, mind has unknowingly hijacked the body and the senses for its own purpose.

In dis-relation with Source, mind will feel insecure. This dis-relation is projected away to protect itself from its insecurity. But its projection of insecurity is the effect of a world of insecure conflict. Now your mind's purpose seems to be to find security in its projection of a body-self idea in an insecure world. That is why your search for security in the world is endlessly frustrating.

---

[38] Society is a collective hunch.
[39] Love, acceptance, understanding etc., are shared symbols of healing because they are about joining.

Using the experience of the senses to prove to ego self that it is subject to and therefore limited by a physical body, you try to make sense out of the experience of your confusion. And you use the only tool that seems available to you; the body the mind uses to deceive itself. How does one dispute the body's fleeting experience of pleasure and pain, not to mention everything the five senses seem to give you?! Only violation and fear could result from this self-deception. That is why your experience of guilt, anger and despair are reoccurring.

To not know is to think.
To think is through the experience of the senses.
Knowing is other than the experience of the senses.

At one time you knew, but you do not remember this.[40] You say "I know" all the time, but all you are doing is perceiving ... all the time! Your mind has become tolerant to the experience of a sensual intoxication you can't understand. You actually believe that you are subject to the body's external reality of change. Because mind perceives itself to be a body it is not, you experience birth, pain, pleasure, fear, anger, guilt, hunger, sacrifice, sorrow and death as real. However, the experience of change does not belong to mind. It belongs to a body of sensation and perception. Mind does not grasp this self-deception because it is preoccupied with defending the experience of the body's senses as a witness to an ephemeral reality as its home. To think other wise is a threat to the ego's existence; its investment to an ephemeral experience. And this

---

[40] *The Way Home p125*

the ego cannot tolerate. However, the fact of the matter is;

> *You may think you desire what you see.*
> *But you saw what you first desired.*

A mind that confuses effects[41] as cause does not realize the extent of its self-deception. You were not "thrown" into this world through birth.[42] Your mind made a world of space and time to project a body image! This projection is a substitute for your relationship with Source. This confusion is the source of all sickness.

Misuse of Power

> *You believe in what you made*
> *Because it was made by your belief in it.*[43]

You are the power of your creation. However, a mind that perceives itself as separate from its Source of power feels vulnerable to attack, pain and corruption. In an attempt to find safety from its own confusion, your mind projected an image into its void of space and time, manifested as an ephemeral vehicle you call your body. However, the body's nature is change and therefore incapable of

---

[41] Including birth to death, everything you experience is an effect of a greater cause.

[42] As noted by Martin Heidegger's existential philosophy, the only conclusion a *subjective individual* could come to in the light of an existence in which everything is ever-changing is that, "what is" is a decision to make movement and noise a meaningful choice to one's self.

[43] A Course In Miracles.

providing a lasting experience of peace and contentment. The separated mind fails to find the safety it desires, finding instead the pain and corruption it tries to avoid.

Only if you believe in a body as your identity can you experience being alone, hurt, angry and afraid.

Your experience of pain and corruption within the limits of your identification with a body, you think, needs to be defended because your investment in it, you think, is your safety. Yet, it will never protect you from the very pain and corruption it causes. Your defense of this contradiction is an attack on your ability to have peace of mind. Because you do not see the mind as separate from bodily conditions, your mind will impose upon the body, as if it is to be your savior from your dilemma, one solution after another. Yet, it will never save you from it's corruption. The result is emotional and physical stress on the body you seem to be.

When you give the body goals it cannot reach
You experience anger, guilt and fear.

Misuse of power is always the disposition of *a frustrated learner* because they are trying to learn an impossible lesson. The body, being a limitation, cannot live up to the demands of a mind confused about itself. It cannot fix mind's problem. Mind's problem is the belief it is something it is not. In your deception does your mind try over and over again to use its effect (the body) to save the cause (the mind that made the problem). How can the body being mind's primary deception save it from its deception?

Your attempt to find comfort, peace and self esteem through a body for the mind can only give you fleeting moments of pleasure, pain and a shallow happiness before it dies.

However, you are not the temporary body you try to identify with. The cause of mind's problem still remains as *an error in thought,* a perceived disconnection from Source. The body is merely the effect of mind's problem, not its cause, nor can it be its solution. All your attempts to find meaningful connections through a body-self idea are in the end, futile substitutions.[44] This is why the body is mind's greatest self-deception. Beyond this confusion, Mind is experienced as eternally changeless.

You Experience What You Believe

How far do you have to step in until you realize
"I am not projecting a world from a body
I am also projecting a body."

Through the experience of a body there seems to be an external world. Your belief in a perceived separation from Source will be a projection outside of mind. You seem to be wired to project rather than reflect. Unknown to you, you project your confusion as a world. You seem to be born, but it is mind's projection of separation. The entire world is in your mind,[45] witnessing to division, multiplication and

---

[44] Meaningful connections through relationships can be found, but if they are investments for peace of mind, they become reasons to believe that abandonment, grief and death are real. These are psychological symbols of power that delay peace of mind.

[45] *The Way Home p167-168*

corruption while striving through a body to find undying connections that can never be. "Till death do we part" ceremonies, funerals, contracts, pledges of honor, ethical, moral and religious absolutes all fall into this category of symbols of power that try to make the temporary sacred.[46]

Mind's search for a place has decided to limit its power "to be" through the five senses. Thus the senses become the means, the measure and therefore the limit of mind's experience for meaning in the ever-changing.[47] What else could mind find in the appearance of the ever-changing but fleeting shadows that come and go?

If you believe that what you believe will save you, then the truth will be viewed as threatening to what you believe.
All defenses against the truth are used to defend the body as true.

Because you suffer from what you believe you are, you can heal. If you do not believe this is true, then healing must wait for your acceptance of this principle while mediating forms[48] for relief are to be used. Remember, you do not believe what you experience, you experience what you believe. Because *no thought leaves its source,* you always

---

[46] The book *Symbols of Power in Philosophy.*

[47] All empirically scientific data is proof that all empirically scientific data are empirical and scientific. In other words, all empirical and scientific data reflect a paradigm that is self-sustaining, not necessarily self-revealing.

[48] The symbols of power you are willing to accept as having healing influence on the body and mind; the placebo effect.

experience the anger, guilt and fear you feel towards someone else. You also experience the love you feel towards someone else.[49]

Allowing any exception to this principle justifies "the victim" as a symbol of power. It limits your perception and thus your ability to change your mind. You do experience the effects of your beliefs. So choose to allow beliefs that heal separation from everyone.[50] It is joining that brings you peace of mind.

Self-Deception as Betrayal

There is no treachery of betrayal except in self-deception!

Because your mind deceives itself for the purpose of identifying as a body, it seems as if the body betrays you when it dies. You may not believe this to be true, however, to grieve the loss of something or someone that was never yours to possess in the first place is a self-deception that hides your self betrayal. You invested poorly for peace of mind. Now you must grieve your mistake.

You are constantly busy with the protection, maintenance, accumulation and continuity of a body. What do you decide and do that does not involve the body? EVERYTHING INVOLVES THE BODY! To "assume" you are a body hides how preoccupied you are with this symbol of limitation. It is an idol of limitation because you place all your

---

[49] All healing relationships are meant to help you remember that you are love.
[50] We are not talking about positive thinking

aspirations of love, success and peace on it. With that, you also reap hate, anger, depression, guilt, pain, hurt, loss and fear! Then you die ... and everything you worked to achieve will be nothing,[51] a memory to someone for a while ... to be forgotten.[52] The life of a body is only dust in the wind and will return to the whirlwind of dust. And yet, you will defend it as "you," to your death ... over and over again. [53]

Knowingly or unknowingly, your mind is always with Source. However, as long as you think the body is you, its end will seem to betray you because it, along with everything else you have embellished and invested in, will perish. No one betrays you but yourself, but even this occurs only in a dream of nothingness ... and this you can change.

> *Cause I'm the spirit of a million voices*
> *Gently whispering in the wind*
> *Moving through the dust of time*
> *Ever -bending to catch your mind*
> *Wake up! Your promise lies within*

Matt Karayan
I Promise

---

[51] Humanism attempts to deny this by believing in the illusion of an evolving social awareness. Human history teaches something different. The book *Symbols of Power in Philosophy.*

[52] Ecclesiastes 2:16. All throughout the book of Ecclesiastes in the bible is the despair of the ephemeral experience.

[53] *The Way Home p183*

Healing as the Changing of Your Mind

There is no miracle in the healing of a body![54] *The miracle is in the changing of your mind about what you think the body is for.* Use the body as an end, as what you think you are and your magical symbols of healing will work sometimes. However, the effect is *always* temporary as long as healing is directed at a body that returns to dust. There is no healing in this. However, when you look without deceit where the real problem was conceived, as an error in thought, healing becomes potential.

hen you can look beyond seeing any "body" as sick, then the body can be an opportunity to heal the mind. Thus the body finds its proper place as *a means* to remind you as to where true healing is to be found ... in the changing of your mind.

Summary

You see only what you wish for.
Out of desire you were born to die.[55]

You are not in the body vessel you think you are. I did not say "The spirit you are resides in the body vessel you are not." I said "You are not in the body vessel you think you are." In other words, "You are not in a body. Your body-self idea is outside of you."

No matter what happens, the body is a part of the cycle of dust. So what are you? What is lasting? What do you hang your beliefs on? Is there

---

[54] "A sickly body does not indicate that a guru is lacking in divine powers any more than life long health necessarily indicates inner illumination." Paramahansa Yogananda, Autobiography of a Yogi p204.

[55] Death is but a symbol for separation, nothing more.

objective meaning outside of your mind when the ever-changing means only what you want it to mean? Is reality yours to select?

Teacher, all of your perceived problems originate from the belief that you are something you are not.[56] The miracle is in the changing of your mind about what you think the body is for. Your only betrayal is in self-deception. And in self-deception you can't see the betrayal of another as their own self-deception.

A mind that sees the insignificance of the body recognizes all relationships as opportunities to join at the level of Mind. If joining is not invested in at the level of form, the body can no longer be misused as a means to justify attack or loss as real. Without these justifications, your mind is free to heal, to communicate joining because it looks beyond the belief in a separation that holds guilt or a grudge. Be free from all idols of belief so you can freely use them as they are; temporary aids to help you rise above them all together.

The body is not right or wrong or good or bad. Nor is there a miracle in the healing of a body! Therefore, it is either an end to nothing or a means to heal your mind. In the meantime you dream a dream, sometimes happy and sometimes sad and scary while you wait for your awakening in Source ... the remembrance of a belonging *from within,* which lies beyond the senses.

---

[56] The illusion of self-esteem. *The Way Home p158-161.*

The Senseless Mind

Have we substituted:

Vision's truth ... with sightless eyes?

The song of love ... lost in fear's disguise?

The taste of home ... for the tasteless pleasures of hell?

Common sense ... with insanity's intoxicating smell?

The touch of healing ... numbed by injury and pain?

But what else could one feel ... when the senseless mind reigns?

Be deceived no more, substitutions they are.
Dismiss their magical spell, you have traveled far.

And in the wake of your destruction
To find it is not there
Is to awaken to your function
Your function to forgive
Finding peace everywhere.

The Earth: Your Reflection

The Earth makes no excuses
It makes no apologies
It is what it is

The Earth makes no promises
It makes no guarantees
It does what it does

Introduction

It is easy to believe that what we see we experience. It is much harder to understand that we experience what we first believed. Through the body, the mind seems to experience a world it is born into, to which it must adapt. At times this world may be appreciated as a God given inspiration ... or grieved as a terrible tragedy. Always at the end is death.

Earth is my Mother, no other, my sanctuary
But earth is my prison, my grave and my mortuary

James Seals
Earth

Simply stated, everything is subject to change. There is nothing that is not subject to change. So your investment for security and identity is in what? The world of appearances deceives the mind that wants to be deceived. Have you set yourself up to believe a lie, experienced that lie as validation for

48

the lie's truth, and then resisted looking at the enormity of your self-deception?[57]

There is no place or object that is holy.
They are all symbolic of something else.

This curriculum is about understanding what the world is for. To understand it you must first forgive the meanings you gave it. When you do, you will understand what the world is for. It is to help you to remember your identity in Source, and nothing more.

---

[57] Denial precedes projection and your projection has been on a grand scale.

Catastrophe or Blessing?

Everything your eyes see and your mind perceives is a contradiction. The contradiction is evident in all you experience; the awe of a rainbow arcing over the destruction left by a tornado; the wonder of a waterfall as a fire burns out of control in the surrounding forest above; the colorful beauty of the coral reef as a shark snatches its prey over it. In order for the mind to maintain its self-deception, it selectively perceives only that which would validate its beliefs and ignores the rest.

The idea that earth occurrences are natural is correct. However, the idea that these occurrences are catastrophes or blessings is incorrect. These observable phenomena demonstrate the way your ephemeral[58] body processes its state of being; as continuous randomization of successive approximations. Because the earth is neither good or bad nor right or wrong, when you take your beliefs and judgments out of it, you will see it reflecting something other than what you believed about it. Teachers who choose to instruct through the dance of Mother Earth, can help by reframing so-called catastrophes as Mother Earth's process.

If you understand, things are the way they are.
If you do not understand, things are the way they are.

Zen proverb

---

[58] As short-lived, transient, brief, temporary, momentary, passing, fleeting and therefore unpredictable.

Trying to Make Sense Out of the Senseless

Trying to make sense out of the senseless is an impossible goal. That is what you are trying to do as your mind uses an ephemeral body (an aspect of Mother Earth), to find grounding in an ephemeral world. This confusion is the source of all your sickness. The result is mind's vain attempt to make adjustment upon adjustment through a body to find a place of safety, shelter and comfort in an ever-changing world. Your witness to your conflicting confusion of contradiction is in your mind's attempt to find a home of security, comfort and justice, while finding many cunning ways to poison the Mother and kill the child. The human condition pollutes the body's drinking water and poisons its food. It wages "just" wars on Mother's children in the name of "ideological truth" and legislates boundaries to possess people, places and things. Is this comfort and justice? No, it's insanity!

Because the mind is determined to succeed in its self-deception through a body to make a home, it complicates its confusion by legislating its insanity through the need for ethics, law, economics and social conduct. Through all this you think you will find some semblance of order, justice and safety. But what you find is a complication of living that breeds worry, stress and violation. Have you built a world to hide in, feeling victim to its process, not knowing you made it?

Progress

The idea of progress is about changing and advancing conditions. The fruit of progress is called the good life, but it never arrives without complication or cost. To live the good life you make adjustments to work, invest, save and build your little kingdom of safety. However, your earth history demonstrates that;

Invention and innovation as advancing conditions aren't wrong ... they are illusion

Be an environmental or social activist if you want to. Just don't accept the erroneous idea that to be happy is about trying to change the world. Happiness in the world is not about social, spiritual or even environmental evolution for planetary progress. Being happy is a state of mind that comes from within regardless of what is happening in the world around you. It's about waking up from a dream that thinks the world is real![59]

Pseudo–Synchronicity

The earth does a dance of random successive approximations. Through your need to make the imprecise meaningful, it is tempting to give sacred meaning to earth's events. For example, "There are more hurricanes than normal." Or, "There are more floods, longer droughts, record snowfalls! Is something significant happening?" Perhaps you want to intervene and redirect the earth's energy[60] through a "collective focus of intention and prayer."[61]

---

[59] The process of change, of becoming, is about the ephemeral. Waking up to what you already are, is about Spirit. *The Way Home p115-120.*
[60] The universe is the miscreation of an idle thought projected out. Energy, being a different form of matter, is nothing but projected thought. *Symbols of Power in Philosophy p174-175, 205-206, 213-216.*

Or maybe, "in the year 2012,[62] the moon is eclipsing[63] at a sacred portal[64] at 6:66 pm,[65] near the time of an equinox or solstice,[66] which happens to be at a time that nine[67] of the planets are aligned in our night sky. This must mean something important!" Or else it is a pseudo-synchronicity the ego uses to spiritualize and make sacred the process of "ashes to ashes, dust to dust."

---

[61] The Harmonic Convergence is a New Age astrological term applied to a planetary alignment, which occurred on August 16–17, 1987. The timing of the Harmonic Convergence correlated with the Mayan calendar, with some consideration also given to European and Asian astrological traditions. The chosen dates have the distinction of marking a planetary alignment with the Sun, Moon and six out of eight planets being "part of the grand trine." The convergence is purported to have "corresponded with a great shift in the earth's energy from warlike to peaceful." It was an opportunity for many to join minds for the purpose of peace.

[62] The end of the Mayan calendar. Maybe the end of the world, or the beginning of Armageddon. Or whatever you like it to mean.

[63] A solar eclipse occurs when the moon passes between the sun and the earth. This symbolizes unification of focus, healing. A lunar eclipse occurs when the moon passes behind the earth so that the earth blocks the sun's rays from reflecting off of the moon. This symbolizes polarity, tension.

[64] Doorway, gateway, entrance.

[65] 666 is the symbol for *the mark of the beast* out of revelations 13:18. It means a lot of things to a lot of theologians. If you are trying to prove something, you could use it to make it mean something for you. By the way, some manuscripts read 616. Yes, I know there is no such time as 6:66 unless it is secretly symbolic for 7:06 which may be a sign for something special. Mae West

No matter what you do *out there*, it's not really happening *out there*. Out there is a reflection of what is happening at the level of your mind. Whether you are talking about disaster or bounty, it is you who try to make the senseless phenomena of the occurrences of random successive approximations, meaningfully real. It is the ego's way to make ever-changing dust, sacred. There is nothing happening out there except what your mind decides it to mean; and what you make it mean you will experience as real to you..

Sacred Magic

If you can see that you have been looking for grounding where it cannot be found, you also come to understand how special gatherings of special events for special reasons in special circles,[68] or special buildings with special people using special rituals with special rocks, incense, feathers and all kinds of other special elements of the earth performed by very special people for special healings, can be made to be *sacred*[69] nonsense.

---

said "1 and 1 is 2; 2 and 2 is 4; and 4 and 4 is 10, if you know how to work it right."

[66] The equinox is when the suns rays directly hit the equator. The solstice is when the earth's tilt is at one extreme or the other, in relation to its revolution around the sun. These all represent the markings of the seasons.

[67] The number 9 represents completion in numerology.

[68] Or "special places" such as spiritual vortexes where energy or life forces are believed to enter the earth from beyond.

[69] *The Way Home p149-151*

Despite ritualizing the ever-changing to make it magical, Mother Earth is the cause of nothing. Therefore, the earth as a causeless effect is not sacred. It is nothing because it was made by you without Source and therefore out of fear. Yes, you can be passionately joyous about the Mother Earth dance in all of her forms, yet, it is out of fear when you grieve or fear death.

Out of fear you select ever-changing people, places and things to be special substitutions to hide behind from Source. *How you decide what is to be sacred and what is not is incomprehensible.* Either it is all sacred or none of it is! The epiphany you experience is not dependent on where you are or what you are doing. It comes from within, what you are when you are ready. I do not deny that people, objects, places and events can stir you to experience a sacred moment out of time, but that can be anything, any place within the readiness of your mind.

In terms of the ever-changing, you are the cause of a miscreation with no effect. There is nothing special about any of those things. It is simply a sacred magical belief ... in nothingness.

What the Earth Really Demonstrates

You believe the world is real because it was made by your belief in it. Your mind is so powerful that it can make a world untrue for you to experience as real.[70] The earth is your projection to hide your guilt from your dis-relation with Source.

---

[70] Just like your mind experiences the tenses of the past and future that are not real to the present tense.

You know this is true because all of your guilt is directly related to your experiences in your world of people things and events. And a very good job you did to hide your guilt from your conscious mind. The catastrophe you see in your world is the catastrophe you refuse to see originating in your mind; the belief you can separate from the Source of your creation. What else could result from this self-deception but an attempt to bury a perpetual separation anxiety to avoid punishment and grief? Yet, you experience anxiety, pain and grief anyway.

What does the Earth teach? It teaches the cycle of impermanence. Birth to death to birth to death is constantly demonstrated through the changes of the seasons.[71] What else could it teach but the obvious? And the body you think you are is but an aspect of the obvious.

The days have changed
But they're all still the same
Just like the changing of the seasons
And the ticking of the clock
Measures what you got
And measures, what you left behind

Matt Karayan
Don't Ever Let Me Go

Your insane interpretation of Mother Earth demonstrates that you are a wanderer lost in a world you made by your belief in it. When it is time for you to release the symbols you made sacred to enslave you, you will be able to use them to show

---

[71] Birth and death are symbolic concepts of the cycle of impermanence. *The Way Home p173-176*

you the way out. Your journey back to Source will be when you see that you are more than the dust of sacred nothingness you call Mother Earth.

Raise to Question

Teachers of the dance, raise to question the way of nature, the circle of life and death, the shedding of a blood sacrifice for absolution. The temptation to explain your projection of the ephemeral by mystifying it as "God's beautiful creation" only makes the dust of change an untouchable sacred idol for the sleepy mind that made it a dream. To select some earth events as "The Will of God"[72] spiritualizes distractions your ego will vigorously defend. This is because all appearances of nature are the illusion of something the ego can make significant to hide behind for its survival. God is not the creator of uncertainty, mystery, change, pleasure, pain and death. We are! Stop the madness of ascribing causes to a god that God does not claim![73] Rather, enjoy what you come upon and play. Just don't invest in its process as something sacred.

Acceptance

You experience self-deception on a daily basis and would be able to see it if you looked honestly at it. Everything that has been built, and will be built will dissolve into sacred nothingness. Acceptance is yielding to the recognition that you made a world unreal to what you are in Truth.

---

[72] How you decide what is to be "The Will of God" and what is not is incomprehensible. It is either "all" The Will of God or none of it is.
[73] *The Way Home p139-144*

The world does nothing to you.
You only thought it did.
Nor do you do anything to the world.
Because you were mistaken about what it is.[74]

The earth is neither good or bad, nor right or wrong. When you take your beliefs and judgments out of it, you can use the earth as a means to reflect something other than your projected guilt that defends a body-self idea to be born to struggle, achieve, experience pleasure and pain and then die again and again. Allow the symbol of Mother to teach you that you are more than the sacred dust of the earth. Allow your projection to reflect your innocence. But first you must understand where innocence comes from.

Summary

Your mind is so powerful that it can make a world untrue for you to experience as real. You do not believe this because you have used the power of your mind to deny the power it is. Give it back to the Spirit of Truth so your mind can be used to remedy your dream of self-deception.

Teachers of the dance, you may think earth history, personal history, culture, sociology, anthropology, etc., plays a part in defining what you are. However, they are an effect of not knowing what you are. They reinforce to teach you what you are not. Do not use symbols and rituals of the earth to enslave the mind to the idea that the grave is your end, for they are an end to nothing. Rather, allow those earth symbols and rituals the

---

[74] A Course in Miracles

opportunity to remind you that what you are lives beyond the dust of time. Then you will know how to appreciate the earth for what it is.

The world you made was made out of an error of thought. Don't think you can find any solution in the world. It was made so you could not escape from your problems. You may think you have choices that make a difference but they are all choices that keep you invested in the world. Your refusal to see the world for what it is keeps you from the only meaningful choice you can make!

Beyond the world you made is the real world. To remember it, is to want only to understand all things as the way they are. Your perception of it must change before it is to be understood. Through forgiveness, you will understand that the reason for the world is to learn how to forgive ... to forgive it the beliefs you have given it.

Until then, you seem to be a wanderer ... moving through the dust of time and the void of space. Therefore, enjoy the rainbow, the water fall and the sunset. Dance around the fire that symbolizes your purification, your initiation to your next step. Feel the exhilarating power of a thunderstorm. Gaze at the wonders of the zodiac. And when you remember them to be but reflections of your abundance in Source, they will be a means to help you awaken. Understand gratitude and you will find contentment through change.

So keep on playing those mind games together
Doing the ritual, dance in the sun

John Lennon
Mind Games

Mathias Karayan

The Concept of Magic

We all been playing those mind games forever
Some kind of druid dude, lifting the veil
Doing the mind guerrilla
Some call it magic, the search for the grail

John Lennon
Mind Games

Introduction

The whole world is smoke and mirrors, a simple
sleight of hand, an illusion of magic, a trick you do
not want to see.

Magic is an ancient practice rooted in rituals,
spiritual divinations,[75] and/or cultural lineage—with
an intention to invoke, manipulate, or manifest
supernatural forces, beings, or entities in the natural
world of the ever-changing ephemeral. It is a term
which has been used to refer to a wide variety of
beliefs and practices, frequently considered
separate from both religion and science.

Magic is the manipulation of people and things
for desired outcomes. As far as self deception goes,
magic is a substitution away from your reliance and
direction in Source. It is a substitution away from
true assistance, your ability to help another re-frame
substitutions (symbols) that limit their ability to look

---

[75] Divination as the art or practice that seeks to foresee
or foretell future events or discover hidden knowledge
usually by the interpretation of omens or by the aid of
supernatural powers

inside where resolution and peace are to be found. As a symbol of power (beliefs you invest in as a way to interpret your world), magic is the slight of hand, a deception to look outside, somewhere else into the world through rituals to influence, manipulate, change people, things and events.

Magic as a Distraction

Magic as a distraction, is the misuse of your mind because it is the focus on solutions external to the mind that made the problem. As self-deception, magic is the manipulation of matter that brings relief sometimes. Because mind over matter is true, the "sometimes" belongs to any attempt to manipulate the external world of ever-changing nothingness. All attempts to manipulate through mind over matter works sometimes. But because your mind is too divided and resistant to be able to generalize that truth to everything, sometimes things work and sometimes they don't.

Magic is different than using your right mind. It isn't necessarily a bad thing when it comes to some mediating factor, placebo effect, etc., for temporary relief. However, ritualistic or repetitive behavior, instead of the exercise in power of your right mind, is not healing or release. It is a time consuming distraction of limitation.

Mediating Forms

How can you correct the error if you do not realize that you are under the spell of your own magic.

Practices such as physical healings, incantations, rituals with religious or pagan symbols, or taking an aspirin for a headache seem to have outcomes that seem to be a cause of healing. However, they are mediating forms (substitutions) for what the mind seems unable to do for itself.

Healing directly through the mind becomes impossible when you demean the power your mind has to heal you directly. So you look out on a world you made out of fear to hide from your fear, seeking aids for healing in forms that do not seem to threaten you. It is your desire for healing that allows these aids to be mediating forms you can accept.

Resistance to Heal

It is within the power of your mind to experience a world you made, and not know you made it.

Any form of healing that is a focus outside of your mind may have temporary results. You know the results are temporary when you engage in a constant search through mediating forms for healing resolve. Your problem seems to be one thing this day and another thing the next day. Why is your search endless? It is endless because the world of form is an outcome removed from the solution; the mind that thought the problem in the first place. Your savior through endless forms of power, seems to appear outside of you for relief because you cannot bring the problem to the cause. The only place where real healing occurs is at the level of changing your mind, not in your manipulation of the world of form.

To tell you that none of your problems are real would be a laughable outrage to those who believe in them. However, it is your thoughts that cause the problems you experience. You think you are affected by the world. But it is a world you projected out of your mind's conflict.[76]

The concept of magic is a placebo effect, a pseudo–synchronicity to the one who needs a savior outside of Source. It provides temporary relief sometimes, but never release. Healing must wait for your readiness to look within to the power of your mind, for that is where lasting healing resides.

Examples of Magical Thinking

As an effect of a conflicted mind, the world was made so you could not find a way out.

The idea that you can judge is magical thinking. The idea that reality is yours to select is magical thinking. When it comes to the world of change, all the facts and outcomes are unknown. Empirical facts based on an ever-changing world has predictable outcomes. But the are all educated guesses of insignificance.

To believe God participates in the dream you made involves the magic of faith, hope[77] and prayer to change God's mind. No matter how humble or selfless your prayer might be for yourself or another, if it is not praying to conform your will to the Will of

---

[76] It is true that you made the world you see. And yet, you can't control it.

[77] Those who know do not need faith and hope. Those who perceive seem to need faith and hope. Yet, faith and hope about tomorrow out of a fearful perception of the past does not allow you to live in the only place peace can be found; in the eternal present.

Source,[78] it is magical thinking. It is not Source's Will that needs to change. It is yours!

Here's a tough one. The manipulation of matter called miracles is an example of magical thinking. Though placebo effects of physical healing demonstrate *mind over matter*, your mind is too divided and resistant to be able to practice that principle consistently. Because you made yourself sick, you can undo it. What is the magic in that?

Hypothetical thinking of possibility[79] is magical thinking. It is the language of tenses, the elusive experience of the tenses that are not real to this present moment.

Putting your thinking into dualistic thoughts[80] of good and bad, ideologies, isms and everything that comes from comparing and contrasting is magical thinking. It is your mind's way to try to make understandable the dream that is a slight of handl.

The Magic of Pseudo-Synchronicity

Pseudo-synchronicity is the magical belief in the coincidence of events as having a purposeful connection. This temptation is to make the dream of events significant (sacred). And because of your desire to want to believe that magic works, in the world of pseudo-synchronicity[81] stuff just happens that you selectively want to believe as magic at work. Although magic can be intriguing, the temptation for self deception here is massive. Magic cannot bring resolve to your mind's conflict. It does not address the source of your problem; the mind

[78] *Awakening to the Christ within p244-252*
[79] *Symbols of Power in Philosophy p27-34*
[80] *Symbols of Power in Philosophy p35-49*
[81] *Symbols of Power in Metaphysics p52-55*
64

that made it.[82] What seems to be purposeful significance of one event coinciding or following another is about your mind wanting importance in the experience of a particular event.

"When you are ready the teacher appears" is not a statement of synchronicity. It is a statement of your mind's readiness to take on what is next. The form presented as next is what your mind is ready to accept. A coincidence of events has value not in the event itself, but in the readiness of your mind to remind you of the transcendent nature of your mind, beyond the event itself. There is no magical correlation. Again, correlations of ever-changing nothingness is your mind's way to try to make magically understandable (sacred), the dream that is not true.

Until each and every event is about the call to awaken from the dream, it is smoke and mirror magic, a delay to reinforce the dream as real. You can dance through each event with joy not because they are real, but because they are not real.

Summary

That the world will save itself from its problems is one of the great obsessions from the beginning of time. History demonstrates that the world is the unsuccessful attempt to save itself from itself.

To look for a savior outside of Source is a delay tactic of placing reliance on you alone. It is the manipulation and making sacred of form for desired outcomes that delays your remembering of where your journey lies. It is smoke and mirror magic that

---

[82] *The Way Home P149-151*

tricks you into believing the world you dream can save you from the world you dream.

Teacher, because sickness is of the mind, so is healing. When your student is afraid to heal, mediating forms the mind can accept will appear. These forms used for relief are not right or wrong or good or bad. They are tangible forms for relief they can accept at that time. *True assistance* is recognizing the mediating forms presented as opportunities to go beyond what those forms represent.

Healer, though these mediating forms are temporary, you can use these aids as steps towards awakening. To be able to use another's symbols is the communication of joining with them. But don't take them as real or you will be as lost as they are!

Shaman, allow no symbol or form of ritual to be a delay to you and your student's journey home.

Magician, remove the smoke and mirror from your eyes so you can see what is behind the curtain.[83] The ever-changing is but a veil to delay your reminder of where the changeless awaits your remembrance.

---

[83] Not unlike the curtain which the Wizard of Oz hid behind while the five travelers interacted with a projection ... until Toto sniffed it out.

Cultures of Lore

The one thing history teaches
Is that we don't learn from it

Introduction

Don't believe that certain cultures of the past were any more advanced or special than the age of today! Those are just romantic fictions. Nor do you want to believe that our world consciousness seemingly growing out of this particular stone age of our anthropological[84] and archaeological[85] history, has been the only one. Because the passing of time can erase and leave no trace of cultures previous to us, the door is open to endless speculation.

Romanticizing the Past

One may romanticize past cultures as having had more information about the wholeness of spiritual healing. However, if this information had been personalized into the core of the people, if they had lived the information they possessed, they never would have lost it! Today, like days past, we are witnesses to the loss of what true healing is about.

---

[84] Anthropology is the systematic study of humanity, with the goal of understanding our evolutionary origins, our distinctiveness as a species, and the great diversity in our forms of social existence across the world and through time.
[85] Archaeology is the science of studying past human life through the excavation and analysis of artifacts, soils, and cultural processes.

The world we know is thinking with a hand-me-down brain.
Insane because it bubbles like the rain causes puddles.

We can't walk so we must sit
While the world goes on and on
Thinking with a hand me down brain

James Seals & Dash Crofts
Hand Me Down Shoe

Do we make cultures and people of other times something different and therefore special? It is tempting to idolize certain people and attribute advanced characteristics to them and therefore make history seem real. Yet, history teaches that it is the nature of the human condition to repeat its destiny until you rise above it all together.[86] Where is that noble savage when you need him?

The Illusion of Progress

The world of progress is smoke and mirror substitutions distracting you from waking up.
You're still spinning in the mud.

Depending on your perspective, you can see in many ways how human kind is progressing forward. Yet, the lesson that history teaches is that we don't learn from it.

It is erroneous to measure an evolution of awareness out of economic, medical and technical

---

[86] This is what the book *Symbols of Power in Philosophy* is all about.

achievements. Nor is the comfort of your body a measure of evolving. These achievements have also been used to find better ways to accumulate power and kill bodies. And the ability to proselytize freedom and democracy easily hides the human condition of personal interests and greed. Without the power you are in Source, "all your mind can do is seemingly divide and subdivide and then attempt to glorify the results."[87]

On an unconscious level there is a desire to remember Source. However, this desire is overshadowed by a desire to ingratiate your body. Because all bodies are born out of guilt, the mind of that body has karma to work through. And instead of doing the work they came here for, they seek substitutions to avoid dealing with a guilt that denies the Truth of your reality in Source. Denial breeds fear. And though you have made amazing technical, medical and scientific progress to save and comfort bodies, human kind continues to use this technology to find clever ways to rape, steal and kill.

The illusion of external change seen as advancement has nothing to do with an evolution of global awareness. This is because the evolution of global awareness is a ruse. No matter how much information is passed down from generations before, for your greater awareness, at birth, you have your karmic debt to pay.[88] And you will pick up where you left off; at your previous death.[89] And so it is, no matter how much information is given for an advanced start, you still have issues individual to

[87] The Disappearance of the Universe, Gary R. Renard p126
[88] *Symbols of Power in Metaphysics p97-109*
[89] *Symbols of Power in Metaphysics p119-144*

you to deal with.[90] That is why the one thing history teaches us is that we don't learn from it. And so it is, oblivious to what the world teaches right in front of us, human kind continues to spin its wheels in the mud.

Dissemination of Information

In the world of change, change has always been the norm while awareness remains with a few. I do not deny that there is a dissemination of logic on a global level that has not been since the dawn of this civilization. So is there a dissemination of misinformation for the mind that wants to be deceived.

We read the world wrong
And say that it deceives us[91]

1) When you try to be something you are not, you are deceived about yourself.
2) The you that you are not, will feel vulnerable.
3) From this vulnerable position is fear made real.
4) To get rid of the fear you made, is a defense that projects it outside of your mind.
5) Now you fear your projection as a form your world presents to your vulnerability as coming at you from the outside.
6) Your defense of your vulnerability against your projection is proof that attack is real.
7) Because you attack through substitutions you use to protect you (words, weapons, etc.), you make the world of events a traumatic event.

---

[90] *Symbols of Power in Metaphysics p134-145*
[91] Rabindranath Tagore (1861-1941) was a Bengali poet, philosopher, artist, playwright, composer and novelist.

8) These unresolved events is the karma you must work out until you forgive it or see it differently.

9) Until then, you are caught in a self-deceptive mental loop of trying to find a "you" in a place it cannot be found.

No matter how much information is out there, your self-deception can't see the truth behind the world of ever-changing appearances. The dissemination of information for meaning makes it difficult for you to see its nothingness.

Summary

Because there never was a past and there will never be a future, our focus need not be about the history of idolized civilizations. Our focus is better served on the opportunity to forgive now.

Let not the illusion of external change be seen as progress. It deceives you into believing in an evolution of awareness. It is not about evolving, it is about waking up.

No matter what the substitutions of progress look like, you are born to undo the guilt you assume. There may be more people becoming aware, but an evolution of consciousness is not what the history of this world demonstrates. The paradox is that it is you alone that is the student to awaken as you teach others to wake up. For no one can awaken you but yourself. And as you awaken through their help, you will find yourself within the experience of One Mind.

We live to wander to die alone.
Until we awaken to the inheritance …
… we all share as One.

Dreaming Realms of Consciousness

Just as you wish,
There are lots of messages in dreams.
There are lots of dreams in messages.

It is within the power of your mind to get lost in them … and not know it.

The Art of Dream Interpretation

Realms of Consciousness

Experiences from Beyond the Dream

Another Dream State

The Time of In-Between

The Art of Dream Interpretation

Dream interpretation can be a creative endeavor when it is used to go beyond the temptation to limit the dream's symbolic meaning to your experience of the ephemeral.[92]

Introduction

Emphasis is often placed on dreams as symbols of hidden personal meanings. This assumption breeds opportunities for misunderstanding and misuse. Dreams can be used as a creative process for inner healing when they are not used to testify to experiences of self-deception. By self-deception, I mean interpretations that reinforce a "self" as a body image in a world of people places and events. To use the dream as a means to go beyond these interpretations is to see the world in a whole new light, a light that reminds you that you are on a journey home. Due to confusion regarding dreams and other experiences mistakenly associated as dreams, clarification is needed.

What a Dream Is

When you are sleeping, a dream is not a related set of circumstances and events. Rather, it is unrelated pieces of projected impressions from memory retained in your unconscious mind. Some of these impressions are stored in the unconscious in order to forget unpleasant experiences. Brought to light through your sleep dream, they are experienced as nightmares. Others are stored over the forgetfulness of time and life-times gone by.

---

[92] Fleeting, short-lived, transitory

As your body sleeps, your mind's self imposed limitations are relaxed. The organizational patterns of memory storage also relax. The stage is set for images from your body memories to loosely flow together in no particular order out of the unconscious. These unrelated images randomly come together to form a series of picture impressions in your sleeping mind.[93] The random recall of these impressions explains the absurdity of your dream experience.

When you awaken with disturbed feelings from some of these impressions, the temptation is to desire a personally meaningful understanding. Too often, an interpreted story line is imposed on these random impressions in an attempt to give meaningful relief to your emotional response. Your range of intense responses associated with these random impressions occurs because of your mind's identification with an investment in an ephemeral body for security. Your discomfort is an effect on the conscious level, which masks your making of an unconscious level. Your unconscious level unknown to you, hides your fear of a mind that has limited itself to the identity of a dream of birth, pleasure, pain and death. To not understand this, allows for all kinds of misinterpretations of what your sleep dreams symbolize.

People will come to you seeking a meaningful resolve to their intense reactions to these random impressions. You can use the absurd dream as an opportunity for them to release unconscious guilt. Because the dream is absurd, it's not about what it

---

[93] Actually, the mind never sleeps but consciousness is temporarily laid to rest.

might mean.[94] But it can be about what it teaches. And it teaches that you can believe the impossible until you wake up from it.

The Making of the Dream

My spirit does not know of limitation.
If I believe in limitation I deny my reality in Spirit.
This is called dreaming.

Because the idea that the limitless can limit itself is a contradiction of thought, your mind enters into conflict. *This conflict can be called a dream state.* In this state, the power of your mind projects its thoughts of conflict to be fearfully real.[95] Whether you seem to be awake or asleep, these thoughts become everything you experience through the life of a body.

You made the world but think the world made you
That's what makes your life in a body a dream

Teacher, how can you see your script for what it is when you are busily trying to teach the impossible, how to make your awake dream make sense?

The Dream's Meaning
Your mind has the ability to bring absurd pictures together, and is often eager to interpret these

---

[94] People don't necessarily believe the sleeping dream is true as much as what they think it might represent.
[95] That you don't recognize that you have projected an experience of a world unreal to Being, is hidden as the unconscious part of your mind.

picture relationships as something meaningful. For example, you can easily interpret a sleeping dream of falling as being out of control; a dream of having an affair is not that you think it will happen as much as it might symbolize an unhappy relationship; a dream in which you are unable to move or call for help may signify vulnerability; the dream of not being prepared for a test may be construed as feelings of inadequacy, fear of failure or lack of confidence regarding your next stage in life. However, the importance of any dream is *only* in the importance that the dreamer gives it.

The meaning of any dream lies with your decision about the dream ... not within the dream itself.

Dream Weaver, how can you assist in dream interpretation for another if you are busy trying to make your awake dream real? To assist another is to help interpret symbols that look beyond the dream.

What Dreams Teach
Everyone has believed that their dream was real ... until they woke up in a sweat thinking with relief "Oh thank goodness, it was just a dream!" What seemed so real asleep can be seen as nonsense when awake. Therefore, the most important thing to remember about dreams is;

Dreams teach that you can believe the impossible

You seemed to experience *the impossible* as real, yet realized your self-deception when you woke up. What you do not realize is that your wakened state is another dream of self-deception.

Consider how you were able to make a world to experience in your sleep dream where none exists. Then remember, dreams teach that you can believe the impossible. While all your sleeping dreams seem to reflect your experience of your waking state, your waking state is but a dream in another form. Whether you sleep or not, your life in a body is but a dream!

✦

Row row row your boat gently down the stream
Merrily merrily merrily merrily
Life is but a dream

You do not believe what you experience, you experience what you decided to believe. Your experience is a deception that blocks your ability to remember what you once knew before believing became a substitute for knowing.[96] You seem to believe what you experience. And what you experience, you believe to be true. You made the dream but think the dream made you. Your self-deception is almost complete![97]

The Power of Dreams

As long as you wander unknowingly in a place not your home, the desire remains strong to make meaningful that which is not your own. This is the power of your dream to deceive. The adept dream interpreter will be aware of the dreamer's tendency to desire a story line that is not so. The interpreter will be able to help the dreamer reinterpret symbols of their dream in a way that helps them transcend or wake up from the dream. For this to be done, the dream interpreter must be able to live outside of the dream, to see the dream for what it is.

*The healed healer stands as a light
Beyond the dream*

Because dreams teach that you can believe the impossible, any interpretation that helps the dreamer approach the awakening from their dream

---

[96] *The Way Home; p125*
[97] The intellect of thinking is an enormous symbol of power. It needs the humility of a proper perspective. Buddha did not realize he was in a dream. He realized he was the maker of the dream.

lends the dream the symbolic power you need, to facilitate healing.

Dream Interpreter, one who has dreams of dying, will use that symbol to justify a fearful world view. Because the dream interpreter understands that all symbols are open to reframing, that which was once interpreted as fear of death can be symbolically interpreted and celebrated as that which has to die so something new can take its place in the dreamers mind. This is what a resurrection, an epiphany[98] or a new beginning is all about. Death is always the opportunity for a fresh start. This reframing transfers symbols of resistance, the vulnerability of a body, into symbols of assistance, the opportunity to transcend this vulnerability.

Summary

All symbols of the ephemeral are to be understood within a larger context ... from outside of the dream altogether. Dream interpreter, in order to be able to interpret dreams for healing purposes, remain aware of your propensity to want to believe that your awake dreams are true. Because your sleep dreams and awake dream are both dreams, the interpretations of your client's sleep dreams are no different than the interpretation of your own awake dreams.

What symbol of power used to hold the dreamer within the conflict of his mind, can save him from the lostness of his dream? It is the forgiveness of

---

[98] a sudden revelation, realization, or insight

the dream that never occurred that can save him from the lostness of his dream!

The adept dream interpreter is able to recognize the dream for what it is and thus, clarify symbols of the dream so the client can move towards awakening from the dream altogether. *The fact that all dreams teach that you can believe the impossible is the only value any dream interpretation has. This is the interpreter's guiding principle.*

Sleepy dreamer, lost under the enchantment of your own spell, all your dreams have but one message to teach you; what you made you mistook as real. Your restless sleep dreams and restless awake dreams are rousing you to awaken from the dream altogether.

Dream Weaver, just for you, teach that the dream your student reacted to is of their making. When you remind them that the dream points to a state of mind beyond the dream itself, you help yourself to wake up as well.

Realms of Consciousness

*The mind that lets the body go
Is not limited to space and time*

Introduction

All beliefs about ever-changing forms are symbols of power that limit your mind to a temporary experience.

Because different realms of consciousness are temporary in experience they have their limits. Because they have their limits, they are unknown to the mind free of all limiting thoughts. A free mind knows[99] and is known by Source. Within Source are there no realms of consciousness. However, a mind that thinks (believes), limits its experience of "Being" by projecting an image of an ephemeral body to defend its experience of limits as real. The idea of space and time is the result. When you deny the mind its ability to free itself from body identification, you deny its potential to go beyond any idea of space and time.

Realms of Consciousness

Limiting mind's power results in the experience of seemingly different levels of awareness. These experiences of different levels are summarized here as realms of consciousness.

---

[99] To know and to believe are two different things. To believe is not to know. It is based on doubt. When you do not know what you are, perception of uncertainty reigns. Self-deception is "thinking" you "know" when you don't.

The ephemeral realm is your primary realm of consciousness. It is the realm of shifting and fleeting forms. It is the realm of a self-projected image as matter or form. The staging for this self-projected image is within the confines of space and ever-changing forms measured as time. It is the home of the body you think you are. The experience of this body in space is self validating through its senses. In the ephemeral, empires come and empires go ... yet, nothing happened.

The astral realm is a thought projection of a transparent self through space. Time nor the senses factor in this experience of consciousness because your mind does not identify with a body-self idea that binds itself to the experience of birth and death.

Some consider an out of body experience as the self deception of a hallucination. That would be correct, and so is your ephemeral experience of a body.

The spiritual realm is your inner place of Being in Source. It is your identity beyond your experience of the ephemeral and astral realm. To some it means heaven. Here, there is no duality of an inner or outer world because there is no outer world.

Brushing up against the veil is what this book is about; experiences, miracles, epiphany's that remind you that you are other than a body.

Space

If space is merely the relationship between objects of movement projected by your mind into the void of consciousness, you will find your Self everywhere.

Space is the idea of an image projected by thought into mind's conscious void. Void is the emptiness of nothing. A self-concept based on a physical body is merely an image of your mind's projection nowhere. Your mind is experiencing its beliefs as if they are out there. But, there is no out there. This seems incomprehensible to the mind given over to the denial of its projections.

It is Mind's nature to Create. However, instead of creating like itself, your mind split between the temporal and eternal projects the split as separation. Without the power you are in Source, "all your mind can do is seemingly divide and subdivide and then attempt to glorify the results."

Void becomes identified as quantitative space when objects are measured with distance between them. Nothing is stationary in this universe mind projects. Because all objects move, measurements between objects are in constant flux. Space becomes the relationship of ever shifting distances between the senses of your body and all other objects. The idea of stability is an illusion.

Time

If time is measured by the mind as the linear progression of events of a body, and that you are not a body is why the concept of time is an illusion; then, you will find your Self everywhere ... now.

Though time travel is greatly sensationalized, Mind does not travel in time. It can remember the experience of a yesterday in any present moment, as if it was there in yesterdays present. This is the experience of recollection which is something different than time travel.

Time is an illusion of linear dimension. *It is always a present thought experience,* of a memory. Any recollected memory (the past) can be an anticipation of tomorrows possibility. The anticipation of a future state based on a remembered thought event seems to make time a real life idea. Yet, no matter how you think about it, whether it is a thought gone by or the anticipation of possibility, *each and every experience you have is always experienced in the present moment.*[100]

Like pictures on a wall
Once they stood very tall
Now mark memories out of time
Yes the ticking of the clock
Measures what you got
And measures what you left behind

Matt Karayan
Don't Ever Let Me Go

Self-deception is the experience of a past tense that anticipates a future tense, blocking your awareness of the only tense there is; the present. Your unawareness of the present does not mean it is not there. As a matter of fact, there is no time but the present. There never was and there never will be a past or future. That is why time is an illusion of linear dimension.

---

[100] *Symbols of Power in Philosophy p27-34*

The Projecting of a "self image"

The projection of a self-image as a body is always *away from* the awareness of Source.[101] This projection into mind's void (space) coupled with the marking of changing thought experiences as time, is the making of the wanderer. Though seemingly drifting through realms of consciousness, it is all done in the world of a confused mind as it looks away from Source onto the making of its own experience of confusion in a void of nothingness.

When mind frees itself from the idea of body identification, astral mobility, past body life recollections and visitations *in any present moment,* become potential. This is possible because it is your mind's natural inclination to be free of limiting thoughts of body identity. Your ability to suspend self-imposed limits finds its potential *in the present.* To move beyond these limits is not difficult when you understand that your mind waits for your remembrance of *the eternal present.*

Truth will teach time to give way to Eternity

That you can project a thought of yourself anywhere into your mind's space is nothing. You have unknowingly already done this through the thought of an ephemeral body! That you realize body identification as a limiting concept of time and space is everything.

Signposts

The astral realm is the idea of a self-image projected through space. Many remember the

---

[101] Because denial precedes projection, you are not aware of what you have done.

experience of being somewhere outside of their material or dense body. A common example would be a sense of floating at the ceiling looking down at your body on an operation table during a body or near body death experience. Or moving through the air over uncharted territory.[102]

The astral realm is different from recollection.[103] *Recollection* is a present memory of a past body experience. Many have had the present experience of remembering historical situations of a past body life. Those body life memories that are more readily recollected are because they were significant to your spiritual awakening.

The experience of the astral has nothing to do with the five senses because it is a projection out of the ephemeral realm of the body's senses. Your astral experience is a present experience of an out of body experience. Recollection is a present experience of a past body life memory.

The experience of the astral realm and recollection, allows your mind room to put your physical body into perspective. It is a realization that you are *other than* the experiences of your ephemeral body. With the experience of a projection outside of your body, or a present remembrance of a past body experience, you come to realize there is something about you that is not born to die. You may have a "wow" experience of freedom from a temporary suspension of your limiting beliefs about you as a body. However, these experiences are still removed from your Source of knowing.

---

[102] *Symbols of Power in Metaphysics p205*
[103] This has also been called past life regression or past life experiences.

Not experiencing recollection, astral travel or any other metaphysical experiences does not mean you are missing out or not moving towards waking up. It means you are using other means on your journey to awaken. Let not the seeking of these experiences delay your journey home.

Teachers of Truth

Teachers of truth, remind your students that recollection and the astral realm are just another realm of *temporary* consciousness, a substitute for remembering Source. Don't get caught up in the glamour of the astral. That would be another form of delay.

Everything outside of your center has a temporary purpose; to bring you back to Source. That is the only value anything has.

As you move through space and time
In the realms of your mind
Enjoy the ride

Summary

Looking outside of Source, through the projection of an image into a void of nothingness, realms of consciousness seem to exist. Projections are recognized in relation to external orientation. Most have gotten lost in the cycle of the ephemeral. Some have gotten caught up in the projections of past body life memories and the glamour of the astral. Your experience of these projections witness to the fact that you are other than a body. They also witness to the fact that you can deceive yourself on a grand scale and not know it. Your projections into the void of your mind are not true. Keep moving!

Experiences from Beyond the Dream

Introduction

It is likely that most everyone has experienced astral travel, past body recollections and visitations apart from your ephemeral experience. However, these phenomenon are not always recognized as such due to your misinterpreting these experiences with preconceived notions.

A Relaxed Mind

The frantic world of a racing mind does not know how to rest. It is preoccupied with the needs, desires and the fixed beliefs about a body-self idea. As a result, exhaustion, stress, worry, illness and various other forms of drama occupy the mind, leaving no room for other kinds of experiences.

Because undisciplined thinking is not an aspect of a relaxed mind, the most common time to actualize your potential for astral mobility, past body recollections and visitations to occur, is when you lay your body down to sleep.[104] In the twilight between wake and sleep the mind relaxes its fixed beliefs about everything. Mind drifts into a relaxed state when occurring thoughts are not given consideration.

Parameters of Experience

When you sleep, thoughts that limit experience are relaxed. Wandering thoughts from the unconscious mind are randomly woven together into an experience of the absurd. When you wake and remember them, they are labeled as dreams;

---

[104] This can also happen through meditation.

and rightfully so. They are merely random thoughts with no thematic connection. Dream interpretation works when you find a theme that can tie those absurd thoughts together. It is the theme that heals when you bring transcendent meaning to the absurd. For example, it could be said that your mind is purging unconscious guilt through the absurd.

Other experiences also occur when your mind is in a relaxed state of suspended limitation. These experiences have also been readily labeled without question as dreams. Although the experience was not an absurd story line, your mind's experience of astral travel, past body recollections and visitations are easily mislabeled as the absurd experience of dreaming.

Your determination of mind to deceive itself into believing you are a body only allows for the five senses as parameters of experience. These parameters must be maintained at all cost because they defend the lie your mind has chosen for its security as a body. And the lie is "I am a body begotten of other bodies to beget other bodies." To seriously question this lie is to set your whole kingdom of body investment upside down.

All defenses against Truth are used to defend the body as real.

Because your experience of past life recollections, out of body experiences / astral mobility and visitations are not absurd but make sense, no theme is needed. They are messengers of opportunity that remind you that you are other than the body you dream.

Mind's Propensity for Self-Deception

Fear is a helpful indication that tells you that you have lied to yourself.

Because you have erroneously identified yourself as a body, any experience that *seems* to threaten the body is interpreted fearfully. To protect yourself from the fear of being mistaken about your dream experience that cannot be explained within the parameters of the five senses, your mind will discount the paranormal. The ego's defense is to keep the experience in question out of the question. It prevents your limiting parameters of interpretation from being scrutinized. Besides rationalizing your experiences away as "just a dream," your paranormal experiences can be denied relevance because they cannot be empirically proven. Either way, they have been put out of reach from your ability to use them as a means to question your body-self identity.

You are not the body you think you are. The ego cannot accept this because to expose the fallacy of your world view would threaten the ego's survival as your guide.

Your defense of any interpretation to protect you from fear is witness to the fear you made.

It is paramount that you recognize your mind's propensity to deceive itself with assumptions like "obviously I am a body," and then to experience those assumptions of the senses as self-validating truth.

If you believe what you believe will save you, the Truth will be threatening to what you believe.

And so it is, if you believe your body is your life line, anything to show you it is not will be a threat to your ego that needs the defense of denial of the obvious … right up to the death of the body.

Visitation

"Lord" [asked Mary], "how does the visionary see the vision: with the soul, or with the spirit?" The Savior answered, saying, "It is not with the soul that one sees, nor yet through the spirit, but by the mind which [lies] between the two. This is [what] sees the vision, and it is that by which I am speaking with you now Mary."[105]

Because there is nothing outside of your mind, you do not see a *vision*. You see with *vision* as projected, that which is already in your mind. It is **by the mind which [lies] between the two** because it is the mind that chooses.

Some may call this a mass hallucination experienced by the many, just like the many appearances of Mary the mother of Jesus. However, the world of your senses is one big mass hallucination experienced in the mind as an aspect of many different individual perspectives. Jesus walks with you in your mind. His second coming is in your mind waiting for you to recognize it.[106]

---

[105] The Gospel of Mary Magdalene 10:6-7. *Awakening to the Christ Within p430*
[106] *Awakening to the Christ Within p68-75*

In your sleep dream, you may have a visitation from within your mind. In your awake dream you are always having visitations or encounters with people seemingly "out there," who have something to teach you. As Jesus says, **"The kingdom of God does not come with observation; nor will they say, 'See here!' or 'See there!' For indeed, the kingdom of God is within you."**[107] Or, you are the kingdom God created.[108]

Given this information, your journey is within you to find "You" because there is nothing out there.

Summary

If space is merely the relationship between objects of movement projected by your mind into the void of consciousness, you will find your Self everywhere.

If time is merely a present thought experience recollected and anticipated, you will find your Self everywhere ... now.

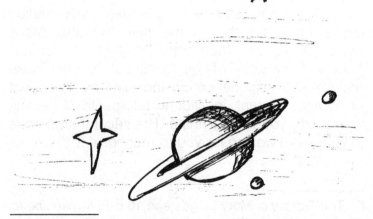

---

[107] Luke 17: 20-21 The New King James Version
[108] *The Way Home p49-52*

Another Dream State

If you allow your mind room for it
There is a realm other than what you experience
through the five senses

Introduction

Experiencing life through the body's senses is like interpreting objects through the distortion of a glass of water. If you do not recognize your body as a means for distortion, you will use it as a tool to try and make sense out of the ever-changing distortion. To try and make sense through a distortion that is not you is a disability which prevents you from remembering what you really are. To forget what you are is to experience a dream state and not know it.

Just because your body seems to be awake does not mean you are

Whatever dream state you seem to be in, is irrelevant if your distortion does not allow you to recognize your natural state. That is why your sleep dreams provide just as much opportunity to awaken as your awake dreams.

Until you awaken to your natural self
Everything is dream interpretation

The Illusion of Disembodied Spirits

Because confusion exists in the mind, disorientation easily occurs to some at the time of their body's death. This results in a state of existence we call ghosts. Ghosts, as aspects of One Mind are separated spirits who resist separating their identity from their physical body.[109]

It is through the limiting experience of a body that time (birth and death) and space (place) seem to have meaning. When your body dies you are released to remember these two to be illusion ... unless you resist mental separation from your body experience. Ghosts are those who refuse to release themselves from total separation of an ephemeral body experience. Caught between two worlds of the same dream, they are free to roam beyond the illusive limits of space and time. Yet, are they caught up in the limiting experience of the ephemeral. This is a conflictually unresolved state of being.

Because ghosts can roam in a different form of dreaming, they frequent places they knew as bodies or "haunt" the place of their exit from their body. That is why some places have an extensive history of being haunted. To the mind limited to the illusion of a body in space and time, the antics of a ghost can be easily interpreted as prankish. And because it is an experience beyond the predictable limits of the five senses, it can easily be distorted as fearful or dismissed as ridiculous.

Unfinished Business

It is believed that ghosts linger because of unfinished business. It is also easy to think ghosts linger because they have interpreted their body death departure as fearfully traumatic. And fearfully

---

[109] Angels are not ghosts. They are messengers of One Mind appearing as projected images in the mind of the dreamer.

traumatic they may seem to be to the one who resisted death (transition). However, whether your transition is fearfully traumatic or not, any unfinished business[110] will bring you back. Unfinished business merely reflects a need to awaken from the dream.

Attempting to chase a ghost out of a familiar haunt without helping to facilitate their awakening from their unfinished business, achieves nothing. Because they are free to roam beyond the illusive limits of space and time, trying to chase them out of anywhere is a fruitless endeavor.

Summary

To the mind confused about what it is, the impossible seems possible. A ghost state reflects mind's propensity to dream the impossible. However, what you dream is not relevant. What matters is awakening from the dream altogether.

Ghosts, in self-deception are dreaming their life through another dream state. Although they will eventually reincarnate to work on unfinished business, they remain in their ghostly state to finish business. Ghosts are no different than you or I, being caught up in a dream state. Just like you, their need is to wake up.

Be patient when they fear the call to heal. Helping a confused spirit move beyond their dream involves getting their attention. Any disembodied spirit's natural desire to awaken will eventually lead them back into the cycle of healing. How is that any different than your journey?

---

[110] Karma.

Mathias Karayan

The Time of In-Between

The time of In-between
Is merely just a dream

A dream of joy, a dream of sorrow
A dream of fear waiting on tomorrow

A dream of hate, a dream of love
A dream from the stars to rise above

What is this dream of in-between?
It is your time ... to dream

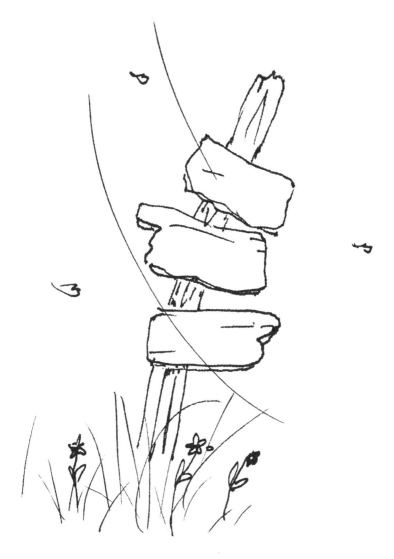

Your interpretation of life events is the script you write. Your script is your destiny, the karma you play out ... until you change your interpretation of your life events.

Karma

Our lives are not our own. From womb to tomb …
… we are bound to others … past and present …
… and by each crime and every kindness …
… we birth our future.

From the movie Cloud Atlas

Karma and Your Destiny

Where is Karma?

The Lash of the Dragon's Tail

Karma and Your Destiny

Because no thought leaves its source, you will experience and act out the thoughts you think. Karma is the effect of what you think. And what you think you will experience as if it is real. Do not underestimate the power of your mind!

Introduction

Your interpretation of life events is the script you write. Your script is your destiny, the karma you play out. In the light of karma, fate is an established inevitable in the world of forms ... until you change your interpretation of your life events. In other words, you will play out your karma until you undo it. Because of your decision against Source,[111] fate is your inevitable journey through a world of meaningless choices. You will play out those conflicting choices until you are decided for the Kingdom that you are.

> *Fate takes one where one goes*
> *The rest it drags along*

Roman Proverb

Karma is neither good nor bad. It's not "payback" for bad behavior or "reward" for good behavior. It is the destiny you play out dependent upon what you think. It is the reflection of your shadow interpreted as your world. It is the projection of the dance you do in your mind. It is nothing but your effect.

---

[111] Or against the Kingdom of God that you are.

Karma crosses apparent body life experiences (lifetimes) as your collection of yesterday's unresolved memories. You are unaware that you make a destiny that is dependent upon what you think because, *denial always precedes projection.*

The Fact of the Matter

Whether you believe in karma or not is irrelevant to the fact that every thought you entertain evokes a response from you. Said in other ways, "He who sows the wind reaps the whirlwind;"[112] or "Do not judge lest you be judged. For in the way you judge, you will be judged; and by your standard of measure, it will be measured to you;"[113] or "To give is to receive is the law of love." Which means, what you give in your thinking you always give to yourself first. "And in the end, the love you take, is equal to the love you make,"[114] is also the law of karma. And "Instant karma's gonna' get you."[115] In other words,

Because no thought leaves its source, every wish finds its fulfillment in the mind that thought it

Karma is the effect of what you think. And what you think you will experience as if it is real. Again, do not underestimate the power of your mind!

Maker of Fate

Because you make your own fate, you are the victim or savior of the fate you make. When you

---

[112] A loose translation of Proverbs 22:8, Hosea 8:7, also James 3:18 & Galatians 6: 7-8.
[113] Matthew 7:1-3.
[114] Lennon & McCartney, the End.
[115] John Lennon, Instant Karma.

become aware of this fact, you can begin the work that cancels your karmic debt. You begin the work when you realize that the problem is in the same place as the solution ... with you!

No matter what countless forms your life seems to take or appears to be, it's all karmic. However, because *complexity of form does not imply complexity of content,* there is a simple solution. This solution goes back to the mind that thought it could get rid of the thoughts it does not like through projection. The simple solution is your ability to change your mind about anything. Until you decide differently you are the self-made victim unknowingly collecting and safeguarding your own fate, to play over and over again in countless forms.[116]

Karma as an Instant Effect

Return to sender, address unknown
No such number, no such zone

Otis Blackwell / Winfield Scott

The letters that show up in your mailbox arrive because they have your address on them. Someone knew how to reach you. The events in your life are like those letters, with one significant difference. Without realizing it, you have mailed them to yourself. Check the handwriting on the envelope. If you look closely, you can tell that it is your own. Open it. Read it. Drink it all in. The

---

[116] This is where blame gets its power to thrive. "What happens to me is your fault" is the ego's way of keeping you in a karmic loop of being a victim of your own thoughts unaware, so you can't begin to interrupt them.

message you send to anyone you always send to yourself first. When you see that *in every circumstance* you are the cause of how you see what you think you understand, then you will see the way to break your karmic cycle.

What you make real in your mind is real to you. What you do not understand is that what is real to you, you first made real in your mind. Every thought has an immediate effect. You always experience *instantly* the thoughts you choose to entertain about everything.

The thoughts you have about another
Is always a gift to you first.
What kind of gift are you giving?[117]

Be conscious of the thoughts you are thinking, other wise you will not be able to to change them. When you have thoughts you do not like, you can either recognize you made them so you can change your mind about them. Or, you can try to avoid them by projecting them away. To project them away is the making of your karma. It's like kicking the can down the road to deal with at a later time … and at a later time, you will have to deal with them.

Despite your attempts to throw away a problem you made by trying to hang it on someone else, it remains in your mind. As a subtle irritation, grievance or sadness it remains as a projection seemingly coming from some unsuspecting

---

[117] You can send yourself messages of hope, peace and love. But if you are sending messages of hate and love, you are a mind in conflict. It is a principle of mind that you cannot serve two masters. *Symbols of Power in Philosophy p252 #2*

wanderer you sometimes think you know. Because you made it, no matter how hard you try, you cannot give it away through blame. You can hide it in your unconscious mind to play it again at a later time in the form of a different problem or in a different body life experience.[118] Or, you can give it to forgiveness as the mindless cause of nothing that it is.[119] There is no escape from karma except through forgiveness. Forgiveness is the only function meaningful in time because it is the only function you can use to collapse time.

Instant Karma at Work

Whatever I do to you I do to myself.
What can I do so I won't suffer?

If your goal is peace of mind, to shorten or collapse time brings you closer to your goal. It is not yours or anybody else's actions that cause you conflict. They are an effect. It is your minds interpretation of those actions that cause you internal conflicts. It is your mind alone that assigns value (meaning) to anything. If you do not know this to be true, you will believe truth is to be found outside of you.[120] And so, just like for everyone else, reality is negotiable. The world demonstrates consistently that everything is subject to

---

[118] Reincarnation. *Symbols of Power in Metaphysics p119-132*

[119] *The Way Home p146*

[120] This is what sacred texts, artifacts, places and sacred relationships are about. They are labeled as "sacred" so they are not seen as idols of faith. Yet, they are substitutes apart from knowing Source directly.

interpretation. That is why Truth or peace of mind is not to be found there. Only self-righteous or self-degrading interpretations of behavior follow from this belief.[121] You will always be found guilty of violating the same standard you set for another.[122] This is karma at work through the *illusion of hypocrisy*

Every mind in conflict is a mind living within the conflict of its own decision.

The threat you feel is not outside of you. It is projected away to be perceived as outside of you. It is a consequence of not recognizing the battle you perceive as going on in the world, [123] is a battle you started in your mind. You may not know it but it is you and you alone who set you up! Blame is counterproductive to the undoing of your karma.

You will not be able to do the work you need to do until until you see clearly and consistently that it is you who set you up. Time collapses whenever effect is brought to the place of cause. And cause is not to be found in the world of space and time. It is in the mind that thought it. When you finally begin to bring the effects of minds cause back to your mind to undo it, you will begin to awaken from our slumber. Until you generalize one lesson learned perfectly to pertain to everything else, you will need

---

[121] The making of the concept of good and evil, right and wrong.

[122] *The Way Home p108-110*

[123] In terms of large scale conflicts, egos may form ideological alliances to battle against other egos who have formed ideological alliances but minds can never join except in peace.

to undo one situation at a time. Because complexity of form does not imply complexity of content, this is the miracle you can do. This is your collapse of time, your end of karma.

Karma and Progression

Karma needs time and space to work itself out. Time and space need karma to justify their existence. When you find that your solution is in the mind that made karma real, time and space become irrelevant.

Karma comes to life in the instant you make an error in thought[124] real to you. The practice of defending your error from the truth guarantees karma's continuity. As far as linear progression goes, an error personalized as hurtful and held onto over time as resentment and guilt, skews your interactions throughout your socialized history.[125] As you react to your interpretations of present tense situations through memories of your past, you make and collect karma. In other words, you plan a destiny based on your interpretations of a past that only exists in your memory. If it seems that you are working through one problem after another to either make someone pay for their "sin" against you or for you to forgive your "sin" against another, you are either adding to or paying off a debt.

Because you do not know how to experience the present tense, you will think in terms of "I should have" or "I should not have" or "you should have" or

---

[124] or misinterpretation.
[125] I am not talking about social conditioning.

"you should not have."[126] Time is what you make when you are not interacting out of a present tense experience.

The Undoing of Karma

Mistakes are nothing but memories made.

Every present conflict has a reason. And every reason makes the conflict irrelevant. If you do not project it away, the reason will stand clear. *The reason for your conflict is to teach you that you saw it wrong.* What else could it be? And because you did not project your error in thought away from your awareness as blame or guilt, you can deal with it. You can ask yourself, "What is going on with me that I took it personally?" I am not trying to exonerate anyone's behavior, which is irrelevant to the point. The point is, I am telling you to ask with a diligence of no exception, "What is going on with me that I took it personally?"

Your misuse of mind causes you to wander through the non-events of time. And non-events they are as you build a world out of a miss-thought to react to. Your unresolved karmic issues are right under your nose in the forms of daily happenings. The lessons you need to learn are given to you daily through the non-events you interpret and experience as conflict. What seems unresolved from the past is simply your conflict in different forms re-emerging in the present.[127] You do not

---

[126] These words symbolize your *attraction to guilt and blame. Symbols of Power in Philosophy p27-34*
[127] Because complexity of form does not imply complexity of content, all of your seemingly different problems have

experience memories. You experience the thought about that memory in the present tense. Therefore, when you change your thoughts about a memory, you can have resolution now.

To heal today's conflict is the way to undo the collection of yesterday's forgotten memories. This makes the idea of working out your karma through the past irrelevant. It does take a vigilance of focus to be consistent in the work you need to do, in the now.

Every ghost of days gone by will haunt the imagination of days to come ... until every problem of days gone by finds its answer now.

Real Forgiveness

Teacher of freedom, it is *real forgiveness* that answers every problem. Forgiveness does not "bite the bullet" for what you think someone has done to you or for what you think you have done. That is not forgiveness. Real forgiveness reminds you that *your unresolved conflicts of what you thought happened were missed opportunities to see your conflicts differently.* To see what happened to you differently is not to justify any behavior as acceptable. But it is an understanding that when love is lacking, ignorance, confusion and fear out of a deep seated sense of loss is everyone's primary motivation. Your conflicts will remain unresolved until you are ready to step up and see them as opportunities. Until then, the making of time is what you do to have time to see your conflicts differently.

_____

the same theme in common and therefore the same solution.

And to see your conflicts differently is the undoing of karma and your collapse of time.

Now is the opportunity to cancel karma. There is no need to work out the past when you continue to make it right under your nose, in the present. Where else would you start? This is the undoing of time.

Confusion tempts you to see life events as opportunities to justify guilt, anger and fear. Guilt, anger and fear bind you to a point of view that says someone needs to be punished. There is no absolution from this point of view because this view involves loss. You are not being asked to play the martyr. However, karma dictates that *as long as you believe someone should pay, you will experience loss. Through your experience of loss, you will be the one who pays. Through real forgiveness you undo the concept of loss.*

Summary

Because no thought leaves the mind that made it, your propensity to judge is hazardous to peace of mind. Because of your propensity to judge against your peace of mind, analyzing the motives of others is risky business. It is you, through the thoughts you choose to entertain, whom you enslave or free.

Teachers of freedom, every conflict has its opportunity for resolution *now*. Forgiveness properly understood is the opportunity to see the real cause of your conflict. You are the source of what you choose to believe. And what you choose you will experience.

Any belief is a symbol of power to either bind you to the seriousness of a world of change, or free you from it. When you believe your misperceptions of anything or anyone to be the truth, that symbol becomes your master. It will demand from you what you believe. Believe in an act of evil and you will fear the world you made. See a call for love instead and you will see opportunity.

You will not escape the injustice you perceive until you understand that you gave it to yourself. When you understand this, you free your mind to perceive it another way. To look again with an open mind at a decision you held fast, is the first step to unmake what you reacted to as personally and meaningfully hurtful.

Your miracle is the opportunity to see that what you have been reacting to was simply a mistake in perception. With perception corrected, guilt, resentment and fear have no reason to be. Rather than remake the same mistake over and over again, now you are free to create!

Where is Karma?

Where is karma, where is its sting?
In the light of forgiveness, the bumble bee sings.

When a thought that can chain
Gives way to freedom's reign
Then it is used to heal
Instead of steal

So where is karma, where is its place?
Like a falling star, it burns through space.

Mathias Karayan

The Lash of the Dragon's Tail

*Oh baby but the god that you been praying to
Is gonna' give you back what you been wishing on
someone else*

Bob Dylan
New Pony

Introduction

Nothing in the world of people, places and things has meaning of itself. The only meaning it has is the meaning each separate mind gives it. Everyone's perception about the world as being an individual experience, different from another, witnesses to the fact that the meaning the world has is the meaning each individual mind gives it. *There are lots of different kinds of dragons running around the world.* Is there a universal truth to be found?

The Frustrated Learner

You may believe that you observe, perceive, evaluate and judge accurately on a consistent basis. But the fact is you perceive and project constantly based solely on what you believe about yourself. Erroneously, it is taught that we are a combination of what the world tells us we are and what we perceive ourselves to be. However, what the world seems to tell you still depends on what you decide the world is telling you. You are caught up in a loop of self deception. There is no escaping this fact until you see it for what it is.

Not only do you interpret what you encounter, you encounter what you desire to see. And, contrary to what you might think, it is always your interpretation that you desire to see.[128]

Because the world as well as your body is ever-changing[129] shadows of nothingness, what you are remains unknown to you, making what you perceive not understandable. And if you do not understand what you are, how can you understand what you see? You can't.

Remember, nothing in the world of people, places and things has meaning of itself. It *all* only means what you want it to mean. And, all your perceptions come from a false sense of a self you don't know. Why else would you misperceive what you think you see on a daily basis?

Did the world deceive you?
Or are you using the world to deceive yourself?

You may want to say that your interpretations were influenced by what happened to you in your past, but that's your interpretation based on what? If your interpretation of your self is mistaken, error in how you perceive your past will result.

You are not a product of your past. But you do experience how you view your past. And trying to make those effects to be as a cause confuses everything. No wonder you are a frustrated student. *The dragon seems real!*

---

[128] The dynamics of selective perception.

[129] Some call it evolving; into what no one knows.

The Dynamics of your Mind as Split

If reality is experienced as the expression of One Mind, there is only One Mind.[130]

If there is only One Mind, then all those individual minds you seem to see out there are you ... an aspect of One Mind.

This is purely intellectual in concept until you experience it as One because, reality is experienced as One Mind.

You constantly perceive, selectively perceive, assume, judge, react to your perceptions, have feelings of guilt, anger and fear that you project to play out on your world of movement and noise. You made the world as a projection away from what you do not want to see on the inside. You do not want to look in because on the unconscious level you vaguely perceive an error made from the point of view of *thinking* that tells you that you are guilty.

Because you are the experience of One Mind, there is no outer world. This is experienced as *knowing*. To *think* is different than *knowing*. It is a *thought* outside of *knowing* and therefore a *thought* outside of Source. Now there seems to be an outer world and an inner world. This is what a split mind is

---

[130] The ego resists the experience of One Mind in the name of an "individual" experience which is the kingdom of its existence. "I will not give up my individual rights!" it demands, as it hides behind a body that will die. However, "God Is" is a statement of inclusive non-duality without opposition.

all about; a battle between the temporal and the eternal that does not know of the temporary.

To *think* is to experience the temporal which is a block from *knowing* the eternal. Outside of your experience with Source is the "thinking" of nothingness. Now the "you" you are not, as if "thrown" out there[131] in confusion, is dealing with a world that isn't. Because of confusion, you have choices out of doubt. Because of doubt, you must think in terms of understanding your world through the opposition of dualistic thinking[132] motivated out of fear. Because of the need to choose, reality seems to be yours to select. You become the maker of a self-esteem to live in a world that isn't. No wonder you are a frustrated student. You are trying to find escape from your problems through the world. Yet, you made the world so you could not escape[133]

Projection makes perception means that what you are looking at "out there" is your inner thoughts projected as an outside world. Your mind is so powerful that you made a place to hide and, made unconscious the one belief you fear the most; *the belief that you could oppose the Will of Source and succeed.* This assumed separation breeds a guilt that needs an absolution from the punishment that guilt demands. To avoid the punishment guilt demands, you made a world of self empowered

---

[131] German philosopher Martin Heidegger (1889–1976) described humans' individual existence as being 'thrown' (*geworfen*) into the world. *Symbols of Power in Philosophy* 19-21, 209-211

[132] *Symbols of Power in Philosophy p35-49*

[133] *The Way Home p71*

symbols (saviors),[134] as a way to get rid of your guilt. But, because *no thought leaves its source* you find no relief from the anger, depression and anxiety that your guilt generates. And, no matter where in the world you search for release, your guilt remains.

All your self-ingratiating or self abasing attempts are idols that you believe in some magical way will complete the self esteem you are not. And because you made a self out of guilt, it is vulnerable to arrogance and humiliation. How can you begin to understand what you perceive if you do not become conscious of your dilemma? *"But the dragon is real!" you protest, "I have been hit by its tail."*

> *You make the victim, you make the hero*
> *You make a road to heaven or hell*
> *You wait on the crossroad of indecision*
> *Lost in the confusion of your own spell*

Attack Made Real

Because you do not know who you are in Source, you perceive through the senses. To perceive is to think and therefore doubt. To doubt is the vulnerability to experience fear. Your vulnerability to fear invites the idea of the need for protection. This need invites the idea that attack is real and could be accomplished. Through your vulnerability as a self esteem, you easily misperceive another's words or behavior as attack not recognizing that it is only a vulnerable self that can interpret words in self-hurting ways. The other person is either extending love or also calling for help just like you, but you

---

[134] All the icons of technology, philosophy, religion, psychology, sociology, economics, history, etc.

miss your opportunity to see their call for help out of your own fearful vulnerability. So you react, justifyingly lash out, out of hurt as if how you perceive what you see is the truth. And while the other may easily be tempted to react to what they perceive as attack coming from you, you miss their call for help by focusing on what appears as attack coming from them. Even though the old saying *sticks and stones may break my bones but words can never hurt me* is true, you perceived someone in a way, as attacking through words a vulnerable self that you are not. *And so you experience the backlash of the dragon's tail.* And it's all happening in your mind!

The Meeting of Confused Minds

All symbols are neutral in meaning. Your belief that movement and noise is something apart from the meaning you give them is denial of true cause and effect. Because of this belief, you do not realize that the only tension you feel comes from the meaning you give anything.

That you may encounter a charged reaction from the behavior of another is undeniable. And you may justify your interpretation of that particular behavior as aggressive. However, a charged encounter does not witness to a negative external influence as much as it witnesses to a clash of arbitrary beliefs between mutually confused minds. Not only are the two of you involved in interpreting your own perceptions of neutral forms for meaning, but you are both involved in an ever-changing context of social meanings that influence your perceptions.

Society as a collective hunch of symbolic meanings does not mean that you are a product of the effect of your social context. It means that you will play out the guilt you bring with you through the form of your particular social context.

When you lack awareness of your ground of Being, what else could you interpret in the encounter but the context of ever-changing confusion? So you both react fearfully to your own interpretation of the other's behaviors. "The way I see it is the right way!" Why? "Because I see it that way." And because attack is the defense of a justified interpretation that says "the other person needs to be punished for what they did to me," attack looks like righteous vindication, the ego's salvation.

Your choices in the ephemeral are always limited dualistic selections between right or wrong, or you like it or you don't like it. Any choice in which someone has to lose for another to gain, indicates a belief in thinking that implies that God takes sides. *So you pray to a god to slay the dragon you made to defend against the Truth.* Because you are not the vulnerable self you made the truth is that no defense is necessary. You cannot be attacked but by yourself. Real forgiveness is the only choice possible because only real forgiveness forgives your perception of everyone.

Summary

Truth needs no defense.[135] But illusion does. As unresolved, your bruised ego argues and ruminates over your righteous assessment of the situation.

---

[135] *The Way Home p28*

You can't resolve it because you projected blame on the other over what you don't want to deal with; that you misperceived the situation and won't admit that you did so in the name of what you want to believe they did or said to you. But what they did or said to you, is not about you, it is about them. Just like what you reacted to is not about them, it is about you. *The dragon you fear is the dragon you made.*

Covering your tracks is projection's denial
You can't see where it's coming from
Even though it's coming from you!

Teacher, do not teach the error of "psychic self-defense" for it is your own projection you defend against. The discomfort you think you experience as coming from someone else is what you first did to yourself. Use your discomfort as an opportunity to look within so you can ask yourself *"What is going on with me that I feel this way towards them?"* Now you approach the place where your error made can be corrected and real forgiveness can be practiced … and they become your teacher. Teacher:

1) Be aware of what you project. By the way, it's all projection.
2) Then you can teach without exception that all so-called negative actions, vibes, energy, gut feelings, first impressions,[136] etc., are merely interpretations of your own projection.

---

[136] As far as selective perception is concerned, how many times do you have to be wrong about first impressions not always being true until you realize that first impressions are not always true?

3) This will bring your client's conflict within the realm of self-resolution because it comes from the mind that made it seem real.
4) This also allows them to see no basis for the idea of attack as meaningfully defendable.

See this without exception and you will free your mind to once again create. To create is to *respond to* a call for help rather than *react against* perceived attack. When your mind is busily defending its reactions against the mirror of its reactions, it cannot see another's call for help.

The beliefs / symbols of power you hold dear take an enormous amount of energy to defend. Your defenses witnesses to the fact that your sacred beliefs are vulnerable to attack.[137] When you no longer need to defend your beliefs your mind is free to create. You are free to join in, dance with, look beyond, rise above whatever life seems to present. What seems to happen to you doesn't matter because it has nothing to do with what "You" truly are. Through real forgiveness you find that place where attack is not real. Now, you are no longer part of the problem but part of the solution.

Here, you realize you made the dragon you fear. You do not have to slay any dragon. Rather, discover that if your mind is powerful enough to make a dragon to believe in, your mind is powerful enough to undo it!

---

[137] And if the sacred is vulnerable to attack, how can they be sacred?

Life's Continuity

The beginning is the place you've already been.

Moving forward is the illusion of wanting to get to the end ... the remembrance of your beginning.

Today is but a ripple of that place in time.

Clarifying the Relationship Between Reincarnation, Karma & Recollection

Any Body Will Do

Nothing's Way

Déjà Vu

Clarifying the Relationship Between Reincarnation, Karma & Recollection

The world is not left by death, but by Truth.

Introduction

Traditional western religious teachings encourage a fearful belief in one life in a body to die and then be judged and sent to some place eternal.[138] There is also those who believe in an ever-changing world of consciousness between birth and death as if this is all there is.[139]

> *Unless God is psycho*
> *There is no God in this world*
> *How could there be?*
> *This world is absurd!*

These two opposing thought systems is a choice between two competing illusions. The apparent need to chose again and again is what keeps you locked into the experience of dualistic thinking.[140] This kind of thinking is what your dream is all about.

---

[138] Hebrews 9:27 states; "And just as it is destined for people to die once, and after this comes judgment," can be said to be true as you re-frame this limiting symbol of power. You free yourself to live when you finally die to ego thinking. The final judgment is awaken and remember yourself as innocent. *The Way Home p183; Awakening to the Christ Within p172-173*

[139] Existential atheists; *Symbols of Power in Philosophy p182-195*

[140] *Symbols of Power in Philosophy p35-49*

Once you have invested in dualistic thinking and thus the experience of ever-changing time, one cycle of a body life experience is just as meaningless as a million cycles. Therefore, whether or not reincarnation, karma and recollection are real, is not the issue. The question for those who believe in reincarnation, karma and recollection is; are they helpful in your spiritual progress[141] towards your awakening from these concepts altogether? Through this perspective do the concepts of reincarnation, karma and recollection have value.

Only one reality is possible and it is experienced as "known." This is other than dualistic thinking where choices are experienced through the senses. Those who identify with the temporal, will experience change and the memory of time in the present moment, as if it is real.

Karma and the Time you Need

Nothing can be kept beyond the death of the body ... except your memory of unresolved (karmic) issues. The ego dictates that it is practical and prudent for you to identify with, invest in and accumulate securities and comfort for the life experience of the body. Ironically, your identification with this investment is your making of karma. Thus does time and space become the necessary conditions needed to undo karma. In other words, your thought separate from Source was a karmic thought outside of Source that needs to be undone. That moment was the making of time as the time you need to undo or forgive that thought. And when

---

[141] This does not imply an evolution of the soul.

your karma is undone your need for time will be no more because,

Your misplaced allegiance to the body is the reason that change, sickness and death become fearful concepts. If you were able to take a look at what all your decisions are based on; the survival of the body as you, you would recognize the insanity of your choices for a security that the body can never give you. Until you face this honestly, the self you are not (ego), is a wanderer in charge of weaving its way through one conflict after another of emotional and physical pain ... sometimes, experiencing fleeting pleasure and shallow happiness until you as a body dies. In truth, the cycles of change witness to neither life nor death.[142] Because, *the change which you are not, provides no meaning for what you are.*

The Interlude between Body Death and Birth

Why think separately of this life and the next when one is born from the last. Time is always too short for those who need it. But for those who love, it lasts forever.

From the Movie Dracula:
The Untold Story (2014)

Your body life on this side of the veil seems to be separate and discontinuous. Each birth and death constitutes the measurement of your life experience in a body. Reincarnation and recollection do not address what happens between these body-lives. These interludes (after body death and before body

---

[142] *The Way Home; p173-176*

birth) are experiences free of the limits of the body's senses of wants, needs and desires. It is the other side of the karmic loop in your dream of reincarnation. When your projected guilt catches up with you, you reincarnate.

Reincarnation is the *ongoing dream* of going into a body again as being part of the cycle of change. It is the same dream because what you are in spirit never dies.[143] But what you invest in as a body, dies over and over again. Death of a body is not the way out. Waking up is. The ongoing dream of birth to death buys you the time you need to wake up. That is why the only purpose of time is to forgive.

What Recollection Is

Recollection or to recall, is a present thought experience of a past body life, remembered by a mind relaxed of self-imposed limits. It is the experience of an illusion looking back. With these limits suspended, your mind has the potential to remember memories of people, places and events of a past body experience as if it were today. Even though it is a memory, it is always remembered in any present moment.

Reincarnation is the continuation of your dream of going into a body again. Because no thought leaves its source, *karma* is the destiny you act out dependent upon how you thought about and thus experienced the symbols of that particular body

_____

[143] The use of the term "past life" is a misnomer. You don't die to live again. "Past body experience" is a more accurate term. You have experienced the illusion of many bodies, but always in the present moment. You only have one life, and that life you experience as One in the Eternal Now.

dream. *Recollection* is remembering the experience of a part of your ongoing dream in the illusion of a past body life.

Recollection's Usefulness

Unresolved memories plans for future possibilities. This blocks your awareness of your present experience in Source.

You have misused your memory for so long that you do not understand that it can be used as an opportunity for you to remember your present experience in Source. Recollection is useful in showing you that your self-imposed limitations from body-birth to body-death are not real to the mind that can skip through the illusion of time through the memories of your mind. Once these limits are recognized as impermanent, your present body experience cannot be taken seriously.

The ephemeral is a limiting experience that has nothing to do with what you are. To recall the memory of a past body experience in a seemingly present body gives your mind a powerful learning opportunity to rethink everything you thought your body is. It can help you take another look at what you have mistaken as true. Recollection aids in the healing of your mind by reminding it of the self-imposed limits it has accepted to unknowingly imprison itself.

Like reincarnation and karma, recollection derives its life from identification with the temporal order of things. Unlike reincarnation and karma, recollection freely skips through different body life times showing you that your self-imposed limitations from body-birth to body-death are not real. Finally, you are presented with a very different choice other than your choices between competing illusions; the opportunity to begin the collapse of time all together. This collapse through your experience of recollection is a reminder that results in a speedup that undoes reincarnation and karma. This is recollections usefulness. But how is this done?

The Part Real Forgiveness Plays
You believe you accomplished the impossible, that you have severed your relationship from Source. This impossible thought is the cause of your dream of guilt. But this is unknown to you because you buried it as unconscious in the memory of times past. You made the body to hide from guilt not knowing that your body was made out of guilt as the ultimate symbol of your separation from Source.

Because the world was made so you could not escape your dilemma, you deal with guilt by either projecting it away as anger and blame or accepting your just punishment through shame and pain. In the world of ever-changing forms, these seem to be your choices. But they are all illusion. The real choice is to forgive your experiences of what you took as real but never was. All of them!

Real forgiveness is like the process of editing a movie. A director needs to edit pieces out that are irrelevant to the story. By reviewing what does and doesn't work, he finds things to edit out on to the cutting floor. In the movie, the editing process culminates in a cohesive story. By removing what distracted from the whole the director is able to present the story he envisioned.

If you compare your life to a movie, your editing process is accomplished through real forgiveness. With its application to every aspect of your karmic story line, you gradually edit out the irrelevant. *The irrelevant is that which has nothing to do with your Eternal Self.* Your speedup is a collapse *of* time, the shortening of the movie called your life. Eventually through real forgiveness you come to realize that you do not have a story to tell because it has all been edited to the cutting floor. In the end, the last illusion is the understanding that there was nothing to forgive. Simply stated; your only focus for redirection is the recognition is that;

Your only function meaningful in time is to forgive

This statement is not intellectual. All consistent applications have their experience. It is to be practiced on your walk through life with everyone you meet![144]

Blocks to Remembering Removed

You may seem to have been moving forward but actually you have been working through the collected memories of your mind. You are moving to undo the first and only error that you buried under all the memories of your mind; the belief you can oppose the Will of Source and succeed. Any recollected memory of a past body experience, properly interpreted is an opportunity to free your mind of self-imposed limits of belief. This becomes a speedup to stir you to remember what you vaguely recall, the experience of One Mind.

---

[144] *Reflections For The Wandering Mind p24-35*

With no story to invest in, you wake up to a reality from the movie you thought was real. When your dream is on the cutting floor after finishing the work of all your forgiveness lessons, your ego is gone. There is no guilting and blaming thoughts that interferes with your experience of knowing what you are. Your need to reincarnate out of guilt to undo guilt is no longer necessary because you no longer have any guilt to undo. You remember the experience of what you really are. Your work of forgiveness undoes the karma that seemed to give you a past to undo in the future. The karmic destiny you made for yourself is undone. With karma gone, there is no past to work out or future to plan. Time is no longer necessary. All there is, is the experience of the Eternal Present.

The View from Your Center

You are not in a body.
The body is outside of you.

Reincarnation is like a hurricane. In the center is peaceful calm. For a brief instant you looked out. For just an instant out of mind, the dazzling ever-changing whirlwind of mystification catches the eye of the mind. With your back to the calm, you walk out into a storm. Disorientation follows and fear becomes a real life experience as you panic about being lost. Not able to remember your way back home, you identify with a body to be your home of safety. Not realizing that your alliance with a body-self idea to find safety from fear actually feeds your fear, you become preoccupied with finding a place to rest so you can hold fear at bay.

I've walked through the darkest forest
I fought through driving rain and snow
While subtle pools of sorrow
Gathered at my feet
Cause without you love
There's nowhere else to be

Forgetting your place of calm, you build your little kingdom of distractions[145] as an attempt to convince yourself that this new body will be your home of safety. You have been trying to convince yourself of this over many body life experiences. However, all your sacred icons will not save you. They are nothing but substitutions that reflect your discontent with what you have settled for. Those in the center see all, know all, and are all.

Coming Home

I'm coming home … coming home
I'm coming home to the place where I belong
But distant roads are calling me
They won't allow my mind to be
Home … where I belong

Coming home is first turning back to look towards your center. Your mind's process is a process of stepping out of the whirlwind of reincarnation one step at a time. It is your journey back to remember your center of calm as your distractions in your current body life call you back in every way possible. As you accept correction to move towards your center, the winds decrease. As the winds

---

[145] The ever-changing world is one big substitution of distractions.

decrease you see more opportunities for joy. It was hard to see those opportunities in the whirlwind of time. In fact, you often saw them as hardship. But now these opportunities become frequent. Like manna from heaven[146] these miracles, epiphanies, are speed-ups that collapse time. They feed your focus for the remembrance of One Mind.

I've been to the highest mountain
I sailed deep into the sea
But there's nothing out there
Nothing there to see
'Cause without you love
There's nowhere else to be[147]

The shedding of your body is not death but the continuity of your karmic dream life in another fashion. Your birthing is the continuation of your same karmic dream life in another body. To shed your investment in *a body image you seem to be,* is to wake up. To no longer identify with a body image as "self," is to have no investment in that which returns to dust. You wake up. The world is not left by death. It is left by waking up.

What is life?
It is the flash of a butterfly in the night
It is the little shadow which runs across the grass
And loses itself in the sunset
There is no death
Only a change of worlds

Crowfoot Chief Seattle

---
[146] Exodus 16, John 6:31-33. *The Way Home p68*
[147] From the song *I'm Coming Home* by Mathias Karayan

Reincarnation and karma reflect your investment in the fleeting. Because change is your investment in what you are not, you *seem* to die again and again and again until you remember the "Eternal I Am." That is the reality you participate in as *knowing.* Recollection is a tool you can use when it reminds you of the changeless "You."

Life's Continuity

The world is not left by death, but by Truth.

Teacher, your experience of the ever-changing suggests that the death of a body is the end of that life. However, within the illusion of a past that never was, and a future that will never be, is an ever present birthing process. All your opportunities to work through the karma of your past body memories is presented to you "now." Although you seem to be a body, born to die over and over again, you have always been "now." All the karmic work you need to do is presented to you "now," in this present body life. When you sit in your center and rest your mind of thoughts that delay, you can experience "you" apart from the body.

Whether it is one body life or a million body lives, the undoing of reincarnation becomes the simple lesson of realizing that you are not the body you seem to be. The continuity of what you are is something more expansive in experience and changeless in the "now."

Any Present Moment Will Do

Any moment you relax the limits your mind puts on the body is an opportunity to experience a memory of a past body experience. Whether it be absurd or not, this can also occur during a sleep dream. This is not time travel. It is only a memory held in your mind throughout the karma of your many body lives. And because recollecting is the experience of a body life memory in any present moment, it witnesses to the fact that time does not exist but in the mind that thinks it.[148]

Because complexity of form docs not imply complexity of content, no matter what form your presenting problem seems to be, reincarnation is the dream of experiencing this same problem over and over again in a different form, in a different life time. Memory makes a past seem real and gone, and therefore untouchable to change. However, because your present conflict is a symbol of an unforgiven past, it is through forgiving your *current* perception of a current issue that undoes time and therefore reincarnation. It is not about what happened that lives on. It is a memory of how you perceived what happened that lives on and is brought to your awareness by a present conflict. Through forgiving your presenting problem, you undo a part of your collective karmic unconscious thoughts. This collapse of time, brings you closer to

---

[148] Though you do not always experience it, you always live in the present. Because your mind is out of control you allow it to wander into experiencing tenses that are not real to the only moment there is; the present moment. *Symbols of Power in Philosophy p27-34; Reflections for the Wandering Mind p33-35*

your awakening. This is what your epiphanies are all about.

Summary

Each event in your present body experience is an opportunity to collapse time, the undoing of your karma. Through real forgiveness, any moment you choose release from the investment of an ephemeral experience is a collapse of time, an expansion of awareness, an arousing from a slumber experienced as an epiphany, a "I never thought about it that way," miracle event.

Your beliefs in symbols of the ever-changing are substitutes that hide what you are. Until you unlearn the lessons that the birth to death cycle provides, you will prepare again to die to the birthing process of reincarnation. It is about forgiving your mistaken perceptions of what you thought the ever-changing was about that releases you from your karmic debt.

There'll come a time when most of us return here
Brought back by our desire to be, a perfect entity
Living through a million years of crying
Until you've realized the Art of Dying

George Harrison
Art of Dying

Any Body Will Do

You will come back until you fulfill your contract. And if the ephemeral is the condition you come back to, the conditions you come back to have value only in relation to helping you fulfill your contract. Other than that, the conditions you come back to are irrelevant.

Introduction

Every unforgiving thought is a karmic contract. It is the destiny you choose. Reincarnation is the dream of returning to an ephemeral body to fulfill your contract, Your particular lessons to fulfill your contract are the forgiving of what you took as real. Do not allow for the thought that you enter a particular body for a particular life style to learn a particular lesson. This error suggests that your scenarios of change in the ephemeral are *particularly important* in order to learn the lesson you are "meant to learn."

The ephemeral is all the same as far as illusion goes. It is not the situation or particular body type you find yourself in that decides your fate. It is your interpretation of any situation that decides how you will journey through the illusion. That one situation of the ephemeral sparks you to forgive is the only value any event has. It is the readiness of your mind that allows for what form[149] will be helpful. And your lesson learned through that particular form allows the presenting form to be irrelevant when the lesson is learned or undone. In other words;

---

[149] Or any situation, event, person. Complexity of form does not imply complexity of content.

It's not what happens that matters.
It's how you think about what happens that matters.
And this you can change!

Your situation is not the determiner of your fate. How you perceive any particular situation is.

Comparing One Illusion to Another

Because the world that seems to be outside of your mind is not separate from your thoughts, there are *no limits* to how you choose to perceive it. Nor is the particular body type you project relevant. If the only meaningful function in time is to forgive your interpretations, there is no real relevance to you being red, yellow, white, or black. Being male or female makes no difference. Being mentally or physically challenged is not a handicap when it comes to forgiving what you need to forgive. Your religious, political, cultural or economic conditions are irrelevant to what you must undo. No matter what you appear to be or the situations you find yourself in, forgiveness levels the playing field because it teaches you that your opportunity for miracles is anywhere, at anytime, in any body form. What does matter is the readiness of your mind to forgive.

When the body becomes the irrelevant factor, there is no more violation to collect karma. When there is no violation, there is no cause that has an effect. With no cause to resolve its effect, there is no karma to forgive and thus, time collapses.

It is the body's eyes that sees differences.
It is the healed mind that does not acknowledge those differences.

Worshiping at the Altar of "Social Conditioning"

Social conditioning is not a cause of your confusion. It is an effect of already being confused.[150]

You are born because of unconscious guilt. You play this guilt out through the environment you find yourself in. Social conditioning is an effect, a way to play out your karma. To try and explain why you are the way you are because of social conditioning has massive contradictions. Only through your denial that you selectively perceive can you delude your self into believing that social conditioning is a significant cause of why you are the way you are. That you learn social niceties, culture and language is true. But to try and make social conditioning a cause of your outlook, attitude and behavior is an attempt to make the world a real cause.

John Locke[151] once postulated "Tabula Rasa,"[152] the theory that at birth the mind is completely empty and unencumbered by innate desire, drives, etc. Consequently, all knowledge is based upon experience. In essence, he believed that we are all born with a blank slate. What you become depends on how your parents and society at large raise you. B F Skinner[153] and other behaviorists took it a step

---

[150] *Symbols of Power in Philosophy p69-89*

[151] English philosopher and political theorist (1632-1704); who began the empiricist tradition that believes all knowledge is derived through the experiences of the senses rather than being innate.

[152] Latin for "blank slate."

[153] American psychologist (1904-1990); developed the theory of operant conditioning; the idea that behavior is determined by its consequences, be they reinforcements

further, stating that if we can make a lion jump through a hoop of fire, if we can make an elephant dance on two legs, if we can make dolphins jump through hoops in the air, if we can make chimpanzees communicate through symbols, then we can turn your child into anything we want through a conditioning of consistent, successive approximations of rewarding desirable behavior after the act, aversive stimuli or punishing undesirable behaviors, and negative reinforcement which is the ignoring of certain behaviors.

However, if you think about when your child was born, even before you had an opportunity to nurture and train them, there was something unique about them from the beginning. Under the guise of a needy or content infant was a personality[154] already all its own. Working with the presentation of this personality, as the child grew you would attempt to reinforce desirable behaviors and attitudes and attempt to extinguish undesirable behaviors and attitudes. Sometimes some of the things you did to modify your child's behaviors seemed to work. Sometimes nothing you did worked. Sometimes behaviors and attitudes would come and go all on their own.

Did you come to this life "innocent" to be conditioned out of it?[155] When did you teach your

---

or punishments. Skinner believed that the only scientific approach to psychology was one that studied behaviors, not internal mental processes.

[154] The illusion of traits, qualities, characteristics, short comings, etc. *Symbols of Power in Philosophy p90-107*

[155] Jean Jacques Rousseau (1712-1778) was a French philosopher, social and political theorist, musician, botanist, and one of the most eloquent writers of the Age of

child the attitude and behaviors of the "terrible twos?" Maybe they brought it with them? Why does one child exhibit that kind of behavior when another child of the same family does not? When did you teach your child to be impulsive about decision making? Maybe they brought it with them? Where did your child's attitude to act out come from? It's tempting to blame it on the mimicking of other preschoolers. Yet, they play out there disposition through mimicking. When did you teach your child to be self-destructive with alcohol and drugs?[156] Maybe they brought it with them? You may say that you modeled bad behavior. How come some children of the same family do not learn it? You may say that one child saw your behavior and decided to do it differently. Where did that sense of choice come from?

Though the contradictions to how you raised your child and how they turned out are enormous, you selectively find witnesses for guilt and blame as explanations for behaviors that have no consistent explanation for how your child turned out. Who taught you to resist this message? Maybe you brought resistance with you? After all these years of education and wisdom writing, how come there is no definitive book on child raising?

No matter what you do, there is an individuality about them that is not yours to mold. They bring this karmic individuality with them through their dream of birth, to undo it. This is their contract. Get over it!

Enlightenment. He believed that children were born innocent and should be protected from society's corrupting effects. *Symbols of Power in Philosophy p69-89*

[156] *Healing the Wound: The Family's Journey through Chemical Dependency p21-26*

If you understand, things are the way they are.
If you do not understand, things are the way they are.[157]

No matter how you think about it and fearfully try to protect your children from self-destruction, just like yourself they have their own journey, a lesson to learn that belongs to that individual alone. In the light of this you can practice real forgiveness. You can forgive yourself for the responsibility you thought was yours but in the bigger picture belonged to the karma of their destiny. In fact, your ability to forgive what you thought was your responsibility, belongs to the karma of your destiny.

Being a parent may seem to give you certain social responsibilities but that does not make you responsible for a child's destiny. Just like your destiny belongs to you alone and not your parents, so does your children's. This is not an excuse for how you parent or a justification to abdicate parental involvement, but it does give you another view as to "what happened," ... and this you can forgive.

Nature vs. Nurture

The "nature" theory of personality development doesn't explain why your child turns out the way they do. Yes, it is true that you can attribute color of eyes, hair, complexion, family mannerisms, physical and mental illnesses, etc., to genetic influence. However, within each family you find totally different personalities and perceptions on how to interpret life situations; being acted out through genetic predispositions.

---

[157] Zen proverb

If you look closely, these personality differences are factors independent of nature and nurture. Your children at birth had something about them that was already them. Just like yourself, all through your child's growing up, no matter what you did to redirect them, they did what they thought. Within the limits of their genetic blue print you may have been involved in behavior modification. However, it was up to each of us to choose our own interpretation of life events. How are you to explain this?

Through the effects of nature and nurture is the work of karma played out. Karma is your story because it is the destiny you made, the destiny for you to undo. Within this context, the controversy of nature vs. nurture becomes irrelevant.

Don't limit a child to your own learning, for they were born in another time.

Rabindranath Tagore

Forgetting What You Really Are

Because Source created you out of Itself, you remain true. The belief that you can oppose The Will of Source and succeed is an error in your thinking that only breeds guilt. And guilt always fears punishment. Out of guilt you dream of incarnating[158] as a way to escape from the punishment you fear. This is the agenda you bring with you at birth. Because denial precedes projection, you forget this whole process. You may argue that social conditioning prevented you from

---

[158] Projecting an image is what dreaming is. You perceive what you project rather than know what you are.

knowing who you are.[159] But the truth is you were born because you don't know the "Self" you are. You were not socially conditioned out of knowing who you are. You were "born" because you forgot. Birth, infancy, and childhood are part of the illusion that our innocence can be taken from us.

Social conditioning is not a cause of confusion. It is an effect of already being confused. It is an effect of the original error to hide from the Truth of the matter. It is a distraction, an explanation, a ruse to avoid dealing with the original error. As a distraction it prevents you from understanding your dilemma.

In the mind of Source you are an expression of love. Any thought apart from that expression projects a body image out of guilt. Because it is your journey to undo guilt, forgiveness is the only function meaningful in time. There is nothing else. One works to make the world real through investing in it, only to dream of dying again. Another works to undo guilt by seeing the world for what it really is. This is what real choice is about. Which do you choose? That is your journey, your destiny to fulfill! And any body, time or place will do within the readiness of your mind.

Any Situation Will Do
The reason body types, sexual identity, genetic makeup, culture, social class and social conditioning are irrelevant is because the lesson for you to learn is the lesson for you to transcend the conditions of these ever-changing forms. The world is just a backdrop, a projection out of guilt to hide

---

[159] The making of the illusion of self-esteem. *Transformational Psychotherapy p55-65*

your guilt. Now it is for you to turn the table on the ego; to use the world of events as opportunities to facilitate the lessons you need, to undo guilt. To believe that these external conditions are particularly important is to deny the simple fact,

Forgiving your interpretation of any situation makes that situation irrelevant. When you finally generalize this lesson to every situation, they all become irrelevant. This is the miracle of undoing what never was.

You proclaim sexual, cultural and personality differences to be significantly important so you can justify the illusion of individuality. You even "honor" these differences as a way to make the world's troubles understandable and therefore solvable.[160] All this explaining is a delay tactic from remembering the experience we all share as One, beyond the differences of a body.

All healing is through joining, the experience of One Mind. Not in analyzing how you are different.
The body's eyes will see differences but it is the healed mind that does not acknowledge them.

Idolizing differences is what breeds the misunderstanding of jealousy, anger, guilt, separation and fear. The undoing of these irrelevant conditions through real forgiveness is what is needed to undo fixed perceptions. Real forgiveness is needed to shift your perception away from the illusion of a hierarchy of individual importance. It is

---

[160] Is there such a thing as a noble open-minded altruistic ego? *The Way Home p145-146*

the understanding of the human condition[161] and what humanity has in common that brings understanding and healing.

The form of your life situation is irrelevant. The only relevance is choosing to see the lesson presented in your particular life situation as an opportunity to heal. One person suffers in a so called easy life of privilege. Another seems to rise above circumstances that others see as hardships. One person uses their interpretation to perceive their life as bitter. Another sees their life with gratitude, as an opportunity to extend love. It is not your life situation that sets you up. It is your readiness to see the opportunity in your particular life situation, to forgive. That is why any life situation will do. The question you want to ask in every situation is; *what do I want to make this situation mean to me?* Remember,

It's not what happens that matters.
It's how you think about what happens that matters.

It is tempting to argue that your life situation is particularly relevant. However, it is your perception of any life situation that decides its relevance. Your miracle reinterprets every situation as an opportunity for you to see it as it always is; a meaningless effect of the mind, mistaken as pleasurably, painfully or fearfully real. Your miracle of forgiving your perception of any given situation shows you that the situation was never the relevant

---

[161] *Symbols of Power in Philosophy and Transformational Psychotherapy.* Are books that address "The human condition."

factor. Thus, you finally used the situation to free your mind of its interpretation. This is the only value any situation has.

Summary

Teacher of healing, though it may appear so, your problems are not coming from outside of you. It is the readiness of your mind that shows you another way to look at it. This is what makes you a healed healer. Now it becomes clear that the only release is through the mind that made the situation seem real. Any situation will do. Any situation that catches your attention is relevant. Only in this does it have value. When you are ready, your teacher will appear. Usually in a form least expected.

If you need to say "There is a reason for this event" then say it and know that it is not about the event. It is the reason that makes the event meaningful. No matter how diverse your presenting problems may appear, they all provide you an opportunity for one reason; to undo your guilt, anger and fear through forgiving your perception of it; so you can wake up![162]

It's not what happens that matters.
It's how you think about what happens that matters.
And this you can change!

Your up-bringing, genetic makeup, social conditioning and life situations are not your problems, they are effects of a greater cause. The cause is a mind confused about what it thinks it is. This is the problem you brought with you through

---

[162] *The Way Home p137-138*

your dream of birth, before you could be socialized into a "so-called" confusion. In fact, confusion about what you are is why you seem to reincarnate!

Because out of confusion you made "nothing" mean something, you can change your mind about it. You can let it remind you without exception that it is your opportunity to remember your innocence ... an innocence that remains safe beyond the nothingness you desired. Choose again.

NOTHING'S WAY [163]

Making something out of nothing
Makes nothing seem like something

When nothing seems like something
You have to do something about it ...
Until you see it as it is ... nothing

And when you do see it as nothing
You can do all without doing

---

[163] *The Way Home p146*

Déjà Vu

When you reach the end, you will find yourself at the beginning. In between the two are experiences you have already traveled.

Introduction

There is nothing mystical about a Déjà Vu experience unless you think an experience other than your current body orientation is something mystical.

A Fleeting Remembrance

In a relaxed state, mind has the potential to recall experiences from your present and past body identities.[164] It also has the ability to project into mind's space.[165] The duration of any of these experiences involves your ability to suspend your limiting thoughts about your current body identity.

A Déjà Vu experience is a fleeting remembrance of a past experience triggered by a present stimulus encounter. It is as if "I've lived this moment before, exactly as it's happening now." It's like a memory and a moment in one. It's illustrated in the expressions "I've done this before" or "I've been here before" or "I feel like I've met you before." But you can't quite put your finger on where you met this person.[166] As you try to savor the experience, it fades. Now only its fleeting memory remains.

---

[164] Recollection
[165] Astral travel
[166] Sometimes because it was in a past body experience.

145

Summary

Any experience you can identify as something beyond the experience of the five senses is a breakthrough. Teacher, do not get side tracked in interpreting the *"wows"* of what those experiences might mean. Instead, allow that wow to remind you that there is a disposition of you as "being" other than the limits your mind has placed on itself through your body.

Section II

Symbols of Power
And
Your Creative Self

Your experience of One Mind is the expression of your creative self … everything else is your brush and canvas

Healing as an Expression of Your Creative Self

Self-Deception: The Primary Block to Expressing Your Creative Self

Communicating From Your Creative Self

Song & Dance

Reflections

Beyond the Veil

Healing as an Expression of Your Creative Self

You will know your creations on this side of the veil. They will remind you that your innocence is already accomplished.

Introduction

As Creation, your experience of reality is known, or shared as One. However, you seem to experience the illusion of an individual self, the experience of a separate reality as self validating. This separate identity denies you the remembrance of the experience of One Mind. From this disposition creating is something you have to learn until you remember the experience of One.

The Search for Release

Minds do not experience need, but bodies do. Your experience of need is justified by your identification with a body as if it is your center of being. Because of this strange situation, your creations[167] are translated as extensions through your body until you remember your creations that flow through the remembrance of One Mind.

A mind cluttered, undecided, and distracted by the needs and limits of a body has to work hard at creating. So the body becomes the mind's means as its extension to create.

Your creations through the body takes many forms that the world of clay provides. You use your hand to move the brush, but it is the mind that

---

[167] Abilities, gifts, talents, etc.

paints the picture. You use your wealth to provide, but it is the mind that perceives the need and the means. You go to war in the name of freedom and peace, but it is the mind of the body of the hand of the gun that pulls the trigger. You fight to defend sacred icons of religion in the name of a body's redemption. But it is the mind that feels the need to be redeemed. You defend or acquire territory you think is yours to possess. That is because you have limited the mind to a body-self idea as its home. In the name of achievement and pleasure, you become addicted to work, alcohol, drugs, food, money, sex, relationships, things, etc., looking for that experience of release. Yet, release is a state of mind. You ingratiate the body with flashy ornaments as attractions. Yet, happiness eludes you. "Somewhere out there it is to be found" you say.

You find temporary relief, but you never find that experience of release. So your search continues as never ending. Because the body's eyes perceive duality, polarity and opposition in everything it looks upon, your mind experiences the conflict of divided goals.[168] How can a cluttered, undecided, divided and distracted mind create as it wanders through the non-events of time?

Because "You Are" the expression of freedom through Source, to limit is to make sick. Your mind is sick, not the body you think you are. It is your mind that has limited its Eternal Creations through temporal forms. This is what sacred scriptures, sacred icons, sacred pictures, sacred beads, sacred rituals and sacred places are all about. To use forms the world provides as a means to express

---

[168] *Symbols of Power in Philosophy p35-49*

and honor your identity as spirit is one thing. To use forms to identify with the world and try to heal a body you are not, is self-deception, an idol of delay.

Any symbol, form of the world, is an idol when used to limit your expression of creation. It is a limit when you believe it can bring you the happiness and security you desire. You may experience temporary relief, a momentary pleasure, a shallow happiness, to search again and again for another idol to satisfy. Decide for any form the world offers as a means of happiness and you will experience depression. When you allow all forms the world presents to be opportunities of release from those forms, you will understand the creative value the world of form has.[169]

Your Primary Need

Because you are not the needs and limits of the body, your creations constantly flow within you looking for expression. You do not recognize this because of your preoccupation with a body that is outside of you. Your distractions and needs are not good or bad, right or wrong. They merely witness to the limits you have given yourself through the ever-changing nothingness of the ephemeral. They are substitutions that block your awareness of your creative spirit. This blocked awareness is projected as needs, beliefs, and judgments of anger, guilt and fear. You will project these limits on your world canvas and mistake them as real.

Even though they are the results of a limiting view through selective judgments, anger, guilt and fear are always perceived as justified. You need to

---

[169] *The Way Home p149-151*

justify them when you fail to see them as an error on your part. Because projection always precedes perception, what you perceive as your world is a mirror of your mind reflected back. Though you do not ask for limitation, what you wish for you always find, not always in the form you desired. For example, you desire pleasure? Within those limits also comes pain. You desire the freedom of a healthy body? Within those parameters is its journey to death. That is why *the body you seem to be, needs to be placed into proper perspective.*

Through the body, you will perceive yourself as lacking. Through this belief in limitation, you will selectively find witnesses of lack. Now you seek for completion in the same place you found lack. How will you find completion in a world you decided demonstrates lack? And because there is no "out there," it's all happening in your mind! This is your mind's distraction to nowhere, its delay.[170] However, the expression of your desire to heal your sense of lack can be translated through your creative spirit.

Willingness to listen is your primary need. The recognize that *you do not know as you think* is a motivation to help you focus on practicing your listening skills. Your ability to exercise discipline of mind depends on your willingness to listen to your internal guide. You know when you are not listening to your guide for peace of mind. You will experience guilt anger and fear. Your primary block to listening is the belief that what you think you see and hear you think you understand! Understand this; the body's eyes perceive conflict. It is your beliefs that

---

[170] Trying to achieve an impossible goal is the definition of a frustrated learner.

are your symbols of sickness. They give you the experiences of anger, guilt and fear. The teacher that listens is open to be reminded by the student to look beyond the symbols of sickness the student presents ... so you teacher can heal. Listen to them.

Be Available

Your willingness to see the truth of what your client represents becomes your door to being a healed healer

You cannot be available to create until you look at what your student truly represents. What they are is what your mind tells you they are, and that is what you first think of you! Your student either symbolizes your innocence or the sickness of your individual self. Delude not yourself, you choose how to perceive your projection. One perception is like a wall, one is like a door. Both views stand symbolically between your inner self and the expression of your creations. One way of seeing keeps you trapped in your perceptual wall of conflict. The other way of seeing is through your perceptual door of forgiveness that sets you free.

Learning to be available to your inner self opens you to experience and express the flow of your creations. Actually, to be available beyond judgment and fear is to tap into the flow of the Creation of One Mind ... in any present moment you choose. Wow! What a resource for free expression. The more you are able to slip beyond beliefs of fear into the flow of free expression, the more you will be able to use the troubles of your life as inspirations through which you express your creations.

Again, your mind is cluttered, distracted and deceived in what it thinks it sees. It always manifests what it first desired. If it is tempted to see a world of conflict not there, it will experience the conflict of its mind projected as a fearful world. This is the power your mind has to either create abundance[171] or experience the projection of confusion, conflict and loss.

Did the world deceive you?
Or are you using the world to deceive yourself?

Being Emptied

Before a vessel can be filled with new wine
The old must be drained

Going through a process?
Take heart, disorientation beckons

None of your old ideas work?
Be glad, you're just being emptied

If the symbols you use, block the expression of your creative process (and it is fear that does this because there is nothing out there), your release to extend and create will involve your willingness to place the body you seem to be into proper perspective. *The body does not demand how things should be. It is your mind that demands how things should be.* The experience of a free mind naturally

---

[171] Abundance is not the collection of things and people (idols) for happiness. Abundance comes from within. *The Way Home p152-154*

expresses its own creations. Engage your passion but don't desire to possess or control outcomes.

Today, I release my body from the demands I put on it ... so it can serve a purpose other than what I think. Then it can serve a purpose for healing.

Trying to control outcomes out of a perceived lack, breeds anxiety, depression, anger and fear. However, to learn what availability means, is the start of your part in the bigger picture. This is the way you participate in the illusion when you do not understand what you think your part should be.

The whole is other than the sum of its parts.[172]
Your part is to be available to the whole.

Healer, it is necessary to release the tendency to want to control healing outcomes. To create is to allow the present moment to be what it is without an idea of what the outcome should be. In this way you participate in the unfolding of, as part of what you create, as inspired through the brush stroke of love.

This world is a blank canvas
And love is what you paint on it

Conflict as a means to Teach Release

A mind unaware of its own decision to limit itself is limited in its ability to create. When you judge, your perceptions are limited to the contradictions of outward appearances. These contradictions of thought take effort to defend. The less beliefs you maintain as to how things should be, the less

---

[172] *Transformational Psychotherapy p17-18*

conflict you will experience. Stop the madness of thinking that what you believe is correct. Your delusion is that *you believe in what you made because it was made by your belief in it.*[173]

Self-righteous anger involves the violation of a thought. Alone as a separate body, you seek the ego alliances of other seemingly separate minds to reinforce the lie that you are justified in your anger. I am not saying that what happened to you is OK. I am saying that whatever justification you use to defend your self-righteous anger, will be the justice of discontent that you will be given back to you as your just due. This will be the karma you add and the extension of the time you will need to undo it! It will plague you until you figure out how to forgive it. And because peace is not established by looking to the world for resolution, changing your mind about how you will interpret the external, is a reflection of an inner process that in-itself express your creative state as creation.

Do not set limits on what you believe can be done through you, so you can accept what can be done for you.

Potential when you Allow

Questions such as "what is my purpose?" and "How am I to be used?" reflect an over active mind looking at the idea of future possibilities. You are only asked to ask "How do I make myself available now?" then listen. You will not be asked to do anything you can't accomplish.

---

[173] A Course in Miracles

So keep on playing those mind games together
Faith in the future out of the now

John Lennon
Mind Games

The hope of a future possibility robs you of your opportunity to be available to create NOW! Because *an open mind does not need to plan,* questions about tomorrow become unimportant. An open mind always sees the opportunity as it arrives NOW. Looking for tomorrow's opportunity causes you to overlook the opportunity presented NOW! An open mind will *always* see the opportunities presented as what they always were, the opportunity you were waiting for NOW! A mind free to create will find Wisdom not of its own, but through the Mind we all know as One.

When you have questions about tomorrow, it is always out of doubt. In the realm of doubt your choices are always between two illusions.[174] There is no choice in this, just apprehension. Though you seem to be choosing between forms in the world, you can never have all the information you need in the world of the fleeting to feel secure.[175] Keep it simple. The healing response would be to use doubt as a means to recognize that "I got ahead of myself." Allow, allow, allow means to forgive. Now you will see the door you face. It open for you. Walk in.[176] Any more than this is mindless thinking.

---

[174] *The Way Home p54-57*
[175] Heraclitus. *Symbols of Power in Philosophy p63*
[176] *The Way Home p190*

Availability

To begin expressing your creative self, there is only one thing you need to do ... be willing, be available.

To create is to share ... to share is to create.
By reinterpreting the propensity to attack into the ability to share, you translate what you have made into what you are. You are Creation!

Teacher, be willing to see the ephemeral as the nothingness it is and you will not perceive attack as anything personal.[177] When you are free to look

---

[177] When you cease interpreting attack as personal, you do not interpret anything as attack, because you see the call for help.

beyond fear, you recognize everyone mistakes the ephemeral as real and takes it personally. So do you. When you stop using all your energy to defend your interpretation of nothing, you allow your creations to manifest themselves through your joyful dance of knowing.

When fear is gone your creations shine

The development of any ability involves your willingness to rethink your beliefs about everything. Your suspension of all beliefs allows you the space to create spontaneously in ways you never imagined. Not only do you extend your inspirations through the paintbrush, you also participate as part of the brush as you allow creation to flow through you. Availability knows no boundaries. It is free beyond any thoughts that want to limit, allowing you the opportunity to meet any need of the moment.

It is not necessary for you to conquer or change or heal the world.[178] By simply being willing to be available, you will be shown what to do.

The Need for Direction

You will have opportunities to study under a variety of teachers, but you do not need to limit yourself to any particular person or institution for direction.[179] However, you do need direction! Because your mind lacks discipline to a greater degree than you want to believe, a daily reminder is

---

[178] *The Way Home p35*
[179] This book is for redirection. There is nothing wrong about having a teacher or guru as an aid for redirection. But if they are not about redirecting you to look inside, to love, they are just another distraction of delay.

most helpful to speed you along your way. Meditations of all sorts are available to help teach your mind the discipline of uninterrupted focus.[180] Allow for a curriculum that is best suited to your needs and style of learning. Yet, if forgiveness is not in the mix, you are just spinning your wheels in the mud of clever sayings.

The practice of application leads to experience

Whatever practice you choose, extend love as your motivation for what you do. This overcomes all fear and teaches you to hear your inner voice. Doubt may be involved in the process of learning but do not fear. Once you start, your outcome is certain. With practice, those vague gut feelings will strengthen into the knowingness of your inner voice. In the beginning, because of lack of awareness, it seems difficult to generalize a lesson learned to other areas of your life.[181] That is why repetition is essential to learning. And I assure you that one day it will dawn on you that complexity of form does not imply complexity of content. The world of form is a complexity of nothingness that is healed by only one thought of forgiveness. That is why;

This world is a blank canvas
And love is what you paint on it

---

[180] *Reflections for the Wandering Mind* is a book for those who want to focus on a unified goal for peace of mind.
[181] To generalize one lesson to others is a collapse of time which is what speed-ups, epiphanies and miracles are all about.

Summary

The body you seem to be is not an end. Like a paintbrush, it is a means of extension ... through which you paint your reflection ... on the canvas of space and time.

Stated simply, to express your creative self involves your participation. Participation simply starts with availability. Your prerequisite for access to your creative self is defenseless availability. Because the world is nothing, there is nothing to defend. NOW you are free to express creation. There is nothing else you need know or do. Your test for which voice you are listening to will be whether or not love or discontent is your motivation.

As you rest in defenseless availability, you gain access to the effortless natural flow of Creation like a hollow reed. This Creative Spirit naturally flowing through you will translate your availability to create through the ever-changing world. Your canvas may be the ever-changing but it is your Spirit within, that envisions, manifests and expresses.[182]

This availability starts with an attitude of meditative discipline. Learning firsthand about the power of your mind through training provides you a freedom from fear that reaches far beyond the distractions and perceived limits of the body. As I have said before, besides your need to recognize that you do not know as you think, *your primary need is to place the body you seem to be into proper perspective.* Any beliefs you use to defend "you" as a body-self-image will be your block to

---

[182] *The Way Home p24-26*

accessing Spirits creative flow. Why? Because Creative Spirit allows rather than confines. Any need to be both creative and in control of outcomes is a contradiction. That is but an example of conflict to a mind split by divided goals.

Healer, teacher, *all sickness is symbolic of your belief that your separation from Source was accomplished*. Because that belief is an error, not only is healing possible, it is inevitable. You deal with the symbols another seemingly individual person presents because those are the symbols that represent their belief in sickness. When you see their symbols as what they are, nothing, you have an opportunity to help them reframe those symbols.

Judgment of another's symbols of power is the unhealed healers dilemma. A healed healer patiently waits, and can create and express healing beyond the limits of what any symbol represents. The opportunity to facilitate healing is to go beyond those symbols altogether. If the other person is not ready for the message, that they are fearfully stuck in defending their symbols of sickness, step back to allow them the suffering they defend.

It is not for you to evaluate the outcome of your gifts. It is for you to give them.

Mathias Karayan

Self-Deception: The Primary Block to Expressing Your Creative Self

Because the guiltless mind needs no protection, your defenses are attempts to protect the guilt you made ... from the Truth.

The Making of Opposition

Defensiveness is nothing more than a reflection of what you do not want to see in yourself. Although it is obscure to you, what you do not want to see is that you harbor a primary belief that you have opposed the Will of Source and succeeded. Because you have not succeeded, your mind is divided in conflict. Because Source does not know of conflict, your mind's solution is powerful enough to deceive itself into believing a dream a state of being that is not real to Source. This split is the making of a self you are not, in a dream that is not. The ego's attempt to confuse and complicate simplicity is enormous. It distracts you by telling the you that is not, that your problem is "out there," in the dream that is not, and then promises through the dream that is not, to show the you, you are not, the way out.

The ego as only a concept of thought, can only exist in the part of your mind that is in conflict. As split, this little kingdom of the ego must constantly defend the illusion of an individual self in a world not true to Source. Only fear can result.

In the world of opposition, fear is dividing. That is why healing your mind is through joining.

The Experience of Self-Deception

You spend your awake life asleep and experience it as real, unaware of how massive your self-deception is. This may seem to be insulting, especially to an empirically minded rationally logical person, yet under the surface of your awareness, like an iceberg, most of what you think remains hidden or unconscious. Your sleep dreams tell you something is there, you just don't know how much.

The ego part of your mind is continually making decisions under the surface as *back door deals* that give you thoughts and feelings you don't always understand. Your unconscious mind is involved in activities that give you subtle feelings about many things. And sometimes you can't explain why you think and feel about something. First impressions may be cherished as gut level truth, but they are often wrong. Your thought life experiences are a mass of contradictions, yet through selective perception deny that it is happening.

The body exemplifies limitation, experiencing *physiological* weakness, sickness, pain and death. Your mind, confused about itself, identifies with the body seeking a protection the body can never give. Through this self-deception of identity, your mind experiences the *psychologically* conflict of confusion. *It is within the power of your mind to experience what it assumes to be true.* This is your mind using the body as a means to deceive itself.

When you lie to yourself, it is easy to believe any lie and not know that you are lying to yourself. The body you are not in a world that is not, is that lie.[183]

---

[183] Betrayal, as it seems from another, always starts with yourself first. *Transformational Psychotherapy p173-175*

Your mind's experience of the effects of its identity with a body-self idea, makes it *almost* impossible to imagine that your mind made the world you see. So now you seem to live pleasure and pain, hot and cold, good and bad, sickness and health, as if they are caused by an outer reality.

A Split Mind

Reality is the experience of One Mind. But this makes no sense to the mind split with divided goals. The split has blocked your experience of One mind making it unknown to you. This is frustrating to the mind trying to understand what One mind means.

The projection of your mind as split looks like a problem outside of you, making for the appearance of an inner and outer world. Maintaining this split requires an enormous amount of energy. With all the substitutions of beliefs you acquire to make meaning out of a world of ever-changing nothingness, you are unable to express your creative mind through Spirit. This block makes for anger, guilt, depression and fear.

You see your problems as "out there" because it seems as if your primary threat to your body is coming from "out there." And so to protect your investment of a body-self idea, all your adaptations are your attempts to reinforce what you are not. Your refusal to see this deception is the dream you make. In your dream you project your split as problems "out there" away from you. Perceived this way, it now seems that you can deal with your many problems using the world of substitutions. Although the world is one big deception, some of the substitutions you use as a means to dismiss your outer world as your reflection of your inner, are psychology, sociology, philosophy, theology, anthropology, politics, economics, etc. These are merely attempts to understand and justify your outer world as real. And,

If you believe what you believe will save you, the truth will scare you. Truth needs no defense, lies do.

Your substitutions may bring some relief some of the time, they may even seem to heal, only to come back hidden from you in a different form. Think about this; you seem to have one hill after another to climb and eventually die on. However, it's the same hill on a seemingly different day. This is because your problem is not "out there;" it was made by your split mind. Self-deceit always involves an enormous amount of effort and fear to maintain … right up to the death of the body. It is smoke and mirror magic to have your mind preoccupied in a place "out there" where solutions to your problems can never be found.

To connect is to heal. To judge is to separate. *You will not find your solution in the world. The world was made so you would not find a way out.* That is why forgiveness is the only function meaningful in time. It heals the split.

Your Reflection as a Symbol of Power

If you allow, you can turn the table on the ego by using every problem you perceive to be an opportunity to remind you where your problem began. In the mind that thought it to be so. Your fundamental shift without exception would be to see the outer world of conflict as a reflection of what is going on in your mind. To begin to recognize that the outer world is merely the reflection of your decision about the inner, is to finally begin your journey back through the maze you made. It is a focus that involves giving up every sacred belief, symbol of power you hold true to defend.

Ego whispers "this will involving giving a lot up." But that is the ego trying to defend against the treat of its existence by fearfully reminding you of the loss you will experience. However, in taking that first step you will come to understand that all of your misery has been under the spell of ego's direction. You are not being asked to give anything up. You are being asked to *exchange*[184] your misery for a direction to peace of mind. One step at a time, you will see that you will be give nothing up but that which you will find has no value to your journey to peace of mind. It is always easy to give up that which you do not want.

You have been vigilant in your struggle to justify and maintain your projection of an outer world. Now you are being asked to do something different. Without exception, you are being asked to see your battle "out there" as an opportunity for peace. It's there, but you have to leave room in your mind to ask to see it. Is it too much to ask you to give up your battle ground for peace of mind?

Your conflicts will continues as long as you believe there are problems "out there" to defend against. The awareness of your dilemma is a mighty companion to help you on your way. Resolution is needed here because resistance is enormous.

---

[184] *Transformational Psychotherapy p126-154, 209-212*

The Solution

All the truth in the world adds up to one big lie

Bob Dylan
Things Have Changed

It is yourself you deceive first. From this point of view how can you know you? That's why you have never ending self-esteem problems.[185] And if you don't know you, how can you look out on a world you made to find a you, you are not?

You are the maker of your dream. You have victimized yourself and become your own enemy. Your way out is to accept the problems you see as the problems you made ... without exception. One exception you permit, allows blame to be a justifiable defense that limits your experience of your creative self. Attack, pain, anger, guilt and fear are devices you made to protect you from waking from the nightmare that justifies attack, pain, anger, guilt and fear as real.

To awaken from your dream is to use the power of your mind to see the outer world as it truly is. It is your reflection. What else could the ever-changing shadows of nothingness be, but that? And because you have mistaken it as something to take personally, it becomes a nothingness you can forgive. Because it has nothing to do with the Spirit you are, you can rise above to join in the memory of your innocence.

To undo your dream, you will have to forgive how you perceive yourself. You will not be able to do that as long as you are in the habit of projecting your

---

[185] *Transformational Psychotherapy p55-65*

self-condemning insecurity on others as betrayal[186] and abandonment.[187] Placing blame[188] denies you the opportunity to forgive because it prevents you from taking responsibility for your projection. Blame is always the self-deception of what you think another has done to you. This defensive position obscures what you have done to yourself. I am not justifying another's insanity. But to not recognize their insanity for what it is, their karmic mistake, is a self-deception to take it personally as your karmic mistake, and not see your insanity in that situation. Therefore, *without exception* say to yourself,

My conflict with anyone is the result of self-deception.

Now, is it time for you to forgive your perception of who you thought your accusers were … and to make amends wherever amends are necessary for your release. This is the proper use of forgiveness.

You cannot forgive the lie you believe, when every lie you believe is used to defend against forgiveness.

Behind every lie you see there is a reason for that lie. That is the truth that freely forgives it. Thus every problem you once defended against as coming from outside of you is your opportunity to question yourself and reflect on your own self-deceit. Now does your enemy become a helper for

---

[186] *Transformational Psychotherapy p173-175*
[187] *Transformational Psychotherapy p117-125*
[188] *Transformational Psychotherapy p106-116*

your journey back to peace. This is your miracle! There is no loss in this, only exchange.

Summary

Who looks outside dreams
Who looks inside awakens

Carl Jung

Your outer world is a projection of what you do not want to see in your inner world. Maintaining this split in your mind requires an enormous amount of energy to defend. It is the cause of all of your ongoing exhaustion, pain and fear. You have no energy to allow for the experience of your creative Self while you are busy defending your interpretations of your projections.

However, the truth is your natural inheritance which is why it needs no defense to maintain. It will flow freely to the mind that honestly and openly relaxes to release the blocks to its awareness.

Because you projected an outer world to experience, you will need to use your reflection to show you that it is an illusion of a mind lost in self-deception. Real forgiveness releases you from the lies you have used against yourself in the name of a world not true. Now are you free to create with the symbols you have empowered to deceive, as an opportunity to free yourself.

Truth encounters no opposition because opposition implies weakness. Only in truth is there real strength.

Mathias Karayan

Communicating From Your Creative Self

Communication is not limited to the small range of channels the world recognizes.[189]

Introduction

There is something that "You Are," other than what you "think" you are. As long as you "think" other than "know" what "You Are," you must use the channels (forms) of communication external to what "You Are." It is self denial to say you know what you are when you base what you think you are on the ever-changing ephemeral.

The idea that you are a body, separate from other bodies, implies the need for "external" forms of communication. All forms of communication are special to you until you remember your identity in One Mind. One Mind is the communication of knowing reality as One. Because it is *experienced* as One, any attempt to explain this becomes an intellectual exercise of external forms of communication. However, as an effect of Creation we all participate as the experience of One Mind. This experience does not require communication as you understand communication to be. Therefore, all forms of specialized communication are temporary in nature to either keep you in your fixed beliefs of separation, or as opportunities through these symbols to remember the experience of One Mind. The healed healer uses symbols of communication

---

[189] A Course In Miracles

to help others remember the shared experience of One mind.

To identify with another's journey is to see beyond their illusion of separation for them, and thus, see beyond yours for you. Whatever problem they present, you can respond to it as the nothingness it is. Of course you take them where they are at with the symbols of sickness they present. But the gift they offer is the reminder that what you took as real, is not so.

Your students, having obscured the truth from themselves must heal themselves, for the truth is in them.[190] Yet, being of One mind, the light of your mind will recognize the light in their mind. This is the basis of all communication. It is a support of the healed healer joining beyond the student's symbols of limitation. Helping them to reframe symbols that limit with words that release, is your goal.

Communication's Creative Purpose

Healer, what appears to come from the outside is the reflection of your thoughts. You are caught in a loop thinking you are listening to another when you are listening to your own interpretation of people, places and things. These are judgments out of your past with future implications that limit your ability to listen. In this way do you get in the way. Shared communication becomes the means to break through this loop.

The creative purpose of communication is to provide information that comes from beyond your

---

[190] Remember; because the body dies, "Heal Thyself" cannot mean heal the body. In the final analysis, sickness and health have nothing to do with a body. **Healing is always about and for the mind.** Page 25.

*self-defeating loop of symbolic meanings. The
primary purpose of all forms of communication is to
remind you to look inward for your answer to all
issues. Why? Because there is no out there!* If the
information conveyed to you or through you does
not remind you to look within for truth, disregard it, it
is another form of delay.

Shared communication that leads you to peace
of mind is truth's standard because truth realized as
peace for all, is shared by all. Yet, it is the many
who do not understand that peace comes from
within rather than from trying to find it in the world.
This book is not truth. It is information channeled via
paper and ink. Perhaps its message will help you
remember your natural state of communication.

Types of Communication

Everything the world is, is a symbol of your belief
in separation. The miracle is your reinterpretation of
these symbols that you allow as joining ... until all
you see is the Creation of One.

To create is to join

What you create you will share or extend as a
unified goal of peace. You cannot do otherwise.
However, a split mind will project conflict rather than
share peace. The interpretation of your world
always takes the forms of what you think. Is there
anything you need to argue about? Can you rise
above your symbol of power that wants to prove
that the separation of differences is real?

Sign language, photography, books, art, graphs,
charts, diagrams, numbers, music, smoke signals,
technology, body language, the internet, snake oil

medicine, mother earth's dance, verbal sounds and even these words are just a few forms that individual minds use to attempt to bridge the space between minds separated by self empowered symbols of the world of nothingness. Because they are symbols of nothingness, they can be undone. That is what the miracle is all about, the undoing or reframing of symbols that limit.

We were talking, about the space between us all
And the people, who hide themselves behind a wall
of illusion

George Harrison
Within You Without You

Verbal and written communication are the most commonly used forms of bridging the space between separate minds. It seems necessary as long as you perceive yourself to be an individual mind in an individual body. From this mindset, words are used as symbols to identify, compare, define, limit, conceptualize, express and judge in order to convey meaning. These symbols create alliances and bridge differences as much as they describe differences and create power struggles.

Healer, any meaning that is presented to you from a seemingly separate individual is always the meaning you give it … unless, and just for a moment, you are not an individual body and thus do not have a story to tell. This is the miracle of creation at work.

The healed healer stands as a light
Beyond the dream

If you are not aware that you are listening to the meanings you impose on words, sounds and behaviors that seem to come from the outside, you will not realize how lost you are in your own projection of a self-limiting experience. Healer, you never react to anyone. You react to your own interpretation of what another's message represents to your mind. This understanding is the miracle that breaks your self-fulfilling loop. All communication that breaks through your projection of your limiting meanings is the expression from your creative self. It is a reinterpretation of your limits of thought that opens you to a glimpse of a Self larger than you. It reminds you that;

All healing is about joining

These epiphanies, miracles, peak experiences, realizations, collapses of time are suspensions of fixed beliefs that help you see things in a different light. It is a momentary expression of your creative self that helps heal your peculiar idea of separation.

Telepathy is a form of communication that shares ideas and thoughts by means other than normal sensory impressions and receptors. You are constantly communicating on a level beyond words and signs. You don't recognize this ability because part of you mind as split has limited itself to communication through an individual body-self idea of sensation and perception, words and signs.

Because the experience of One Mind is your inheritance, Telepathic communication is a glimpse of the Self we all share. It may seem mystically supernatural. But that is only because you have limited yourself from what is natural in communicating from one mind to another.

Telepathy is temporary because it is an experience of communicating as one individual mind to another. Through the experience of One Mind full communication is recognized. There is no other mind.

Because the experience of One Mind is your inheritance, your potential to remember full communication is inevitable. *You meet the conditions for this experience when you selectively perceive only the forms that reflect joining.* Communicating through your creative self involves a willingness to see only commonality and wholeness in everything you look upon. This ability overlooks all thoughts and judgments that would limit your mind to an individual experience of separation.

In the dream, the body's eyes may continue to see differences. But it is the healed mind that does not acknowledge them.

What is the experience of telepathic communication? Like all forms of communication, it is the joining with another through the recognition of thoughts you already share. Here is where real communication is recognized as itself.

An open mind is like a mirror when it sees itself in another.

Channeling is a specialized form of telepathic communication. There are two types of conductors for channeling.

The ***trans-medium*** is passive during the exchange of information. They simply pass it on. Though the trans-medium may be given over as an open channel, that does not mean the source is a pure transmitter. The source's intention is determined by its goal. Is the goal in the message about joining or division?

Any source that does not use symbols of power as a means to release you is about cultivating a dependency as your guide.[191] This is not a pure transmitter. The symbols that lend themselves towards a unified direction of peace of mind are the aids that help you remember your experience of joining.

Your ego wants to sneak in with a message that judges another as lacking so you can feel good about yourself. A pure transmitter's intent is always for joining, not separation. Its healing goal is for you to look within to peace of mind.

The ***intuitive reader*** subjectively participates in the information given to them from the other their client. As a healed healer the intuitive reader is able to reframe their client's symbols in a different light. For example, death can be the death of an old way for the new. All your clients fixed symbols of belief can be reframed as means to transcend them, to make them unnecessary to the client. Seeing their client as One Mind with them, they reflect interpretations of healing; interpretations that facilitate the opportunity for their client to rise above their limiting symbols of belief.

---

[191] This is what cultic leadership is about. *The Way Home* p190

For the intuitive reader, the pressure to pacify for personal gain, to reinforce the client's dependency on the reader, can be so strong that they may compromise the interpretation of their clients presented symbols. Without the understanding of what a healed healer is, the reader all to easily adds their own spin that does not interpret the client's symbols in a way that frees them. Thus, the intuitive reader becomes little more than what appears to be a charlatan.

In your sleep dream, you may have *a visitation.* This is from within your mind. In your awake dream you are always having visitations or encounters with people seemingly "out there," who have something to teach you. Because there is nothing outside of your mind, you do not see a *vision*. But because you project it out of your mind, you see with *vision* what is already in your mind.[192]

If you are centered beyond the lure of the ephemeral, the symbols you interpret for another will reflect opportunities for unity, forgiveness and healing. This principle consistently applied, is what makes you a healed healer.

Physician, Heal Thyself
To interact openly with your client is to look beyond the sickness they present. When you look beyond their sickness to the wholeness they are, you reflect a message of healing. Said another way, when you see your projection in another as the spark you are, you transcend the illusion of space

---

[192] See pg 88-92 in this book.

and time and thus, transcend the sickness that seems to be between the two of you.

The illusion of space is a junk yard in your mind, filled with all the substitutions, limiting beliefs, symbols of power your mind has devised to deceive itself into believing in the experience of an individual reality. The illusion of time is the time you need to clear the junk out of your mind. That is why you can transcend the illusion of space and time that seems to be between you and your client when you are able to see it for what it is, the nothingness that isn't to forgive. The last illusion is the recognition that there was never anything to forgive.

Beyond space is to be everywhere
Beyond time is to be everywhere now

It is the "now" that is the eternal present, the only place you can commune with Creation. And that is your experience of Being as full communication with the Self you are. To see yourself in your client is to move towards the memory of One Mind. This is what is meant by "Physician, heal thyself."

All healing is about joining

This is the experience of the spiritual relationship. With this experience of joining, you can never fully buy into what the world seems to offer.

Receive Your Love Freely

To communicate from your Creative Self is to allow the love that flows through you to be reflected through another. This is what your experience of *no thought leaves its source* is all about; experiencing your reflection of love and forgiveness seemingly from another person that seems to be an aspect of your mind on the "outside" … until you awaken from the dream. Just as you are an aspect of their mind doing the work they need to do, … until they awaken from the dream.

> *As an aspect of my mind*
> *Together we walk in time*
> *Upon a thousand trails it seems*
> *'Til we waken from the dream*

Matt Karayan
The Last Dream

Therefore, any limitation you impose on the message you send, is a message of limitation you send to yourself. This self attack is the making of your karma. And because no thought leaves its source, your karma is always instant. Let all barriers down so you may allow love to flow freely through you to you.

> *You are Creation's effect*
> *What you give is always given to you*

It is only fear that limits your expression of your creative self. Release yourself from the fear of being judged by outcomes. Through your motivation to love, your are a naturally uninhibited channel, limitless in Source. And through all that you do, think and say, receive your love freely. Remember;

It is not for you to evaluate the outcome of your gifts. It is for you to give them.

Summary

Teacher, your idea of a separate identity selectively perceives your experiences as different from everyone else's. However, forgiveness of differences is the joining that transcends the illusion of individual experiences. The form any event takes will be different, it always is. But the experience of healing is understood by all.

Healer, the illusion of different experiences makes it necessary for you to engage in and exchange symbolic meanings. It's called communication. All forms of communication exist because you believe you are a body separate from another body. Though the illusion of space between bodies seems to exist, Mind continues to communicate as One. It is for you to let go of all limiting meanings you have placed between you and your client so those symbols can be reinterpreted to remember the truth of what you both are. You need your client to remind you of this. When you remember Source, external forms of communication are no longer necessary. It's all so simple when you remember that;

This world is a blank canvas
And love is what you paint on it

Spiritual Guides

Spiritual guides symbolize any form outside of you that you believe holds answers or wisdom you don't possess. You have to ask for help, interpret the directions and trust the advice. Yet, if wisdom is your inheritance as Creation, it is accessible to all. It can't be held back, hidden or partially revealed. That Wisdom may seem to be hidden from you is only because you have hidden it from yourself. You perceive a need for spiritual guides as long as you block your experience of a shared reality from your Source of Wisdom.

People who seek spiritual guides can be vulnerable to misdirection and / or cult worship. In working with people who seek spiritual guides, teach them to remember that guides are symbols of knowledge that we all possess. If a guide reminds you to look within for the solution, the place where the problem was made, they are helpful. As a healed healer, use the symbols of power another presents as a means to move beyond all symbols. Your primary symbol of power is as always, the understanding that the only function meaningful in time is forgiveness.

The healed healer stands as a light
Beyond the dream

Mathias Karayan

I Send You

I send you!
I send you on a journey
This journey is one you make in your own way
At your own pace

Until you see where your path begins
You will wander aimlessly and endlessly through space and time
Attracted by innumerable forms of magical symbols

When you desire above all else to awaken from your dream ... to be home
You will be home[193]
For I send you back to You!

---

[193] *The Way Home* p199-201

Mathias Karayan

Song & Dance

When it comes to things to cherish, there are many. For example, the birth of a baby, the accomplishment of a goal, advancement in a job, a raise in pay, the recognition of a job well done, the accumulation of toys, friendship, someone to love, someone saying "I love you" and above all else, the belief in a physical body as "me." Though you might prefer one thing over another, your preference does not make that particular illusion more real.

All illusions are one.
One is not more real than another.

Something that I have personally cherished and strongly identified with when all the economics, politics and theologies of the world seem crazy was the honoring of Mother Earth and Mother Earth teachings.[194]

I love a story around a fire.
I love when Venus greets me in the morning or
  evening sky.
I love a walk through the woods.
I love the change of seasons, the colors of fall, the
  falling leaves, the first snow.
I love the phases of the moon.
I love to float down a wilderness stream.
I love the power of a storm.
I love how Mother Earth knows how to be.

---

[194] *The Way Home p23-26*

Even still, the earth may be evolving, but not into perfection. As "ashes to ashes and dust to dust," Without judgment, in that way it is perfection.

The days have changed
Yet there all still the same
Just like the changing of the seasons
And the ticking of the clock
Measures what you got
And measures - what you left behind[195]

In the light of this, everything the world is, is a dance.

You dance in your slumber
You dance in your dreams.
You dance when you whisper
You dance when you sing.
You dance when you walk
You dance when you run.
You dance with your eyes
You dance when you cry.
You dance to get down
You dance to get high.
You dance to a dirge
You dance when you die.

There isn't anything in this world you do not dance
to ... for this journey through is but one big song
and dance.
So make a nice tune to dance through.
Make it a celebration of life!

---

[195] From the song *Don't Let Me Go*

Reflections

Simply stated, words reflect what you believe. Not only do the words you use symbolize the beliefs you hold dear, you also respond to the meanings you give to words that another uses. Words mean different things to different people. No wonder misunderstanding abounds.

At times, words seem to bring new information to you. Other times, the words you encounter seem to illicit a response or stir an emotional memory. Whether clearly seen or not, your response to any word is a reflection of what was already inside of you. How you respond to your reflection is your expression of what you think of you.

What follows here are symbols of expression known as poetry. Allow the words to remind you of what you have hidden from your view.

The King of In-Between

I am the king of In-Between, of In-Between I am.
You'll never catch the likes of me, keep trying if you can.

The moon is always full
The moon is always new
Depends upon your point of view
Which view will you choose?

I am the king of In-Between, of In-Between I am.
You'll never catch the likes of me, keep trying if you can.

Shadows out of light
Darkness breaking through
It's always In-Between
No matter what you do

I am the king of In-Between, of In-Between I am.
You'll never catch the likes of me, keep trying if you can.

Each time of In-between
Casts a shadow or a spell
Which do you choose?
Is it heaven or is it hell?

I am the king of In-Between, of In-Between I am.
You'll never catch the likes of me, keep trying if you can.

Mathias Karayan

Each day is like another
Yet none are quite the same
Each moment you find your rest
No paradox remains

I am the king of In-Between, of In-Between I am.
You'll never catch the likes of me, keep trying if you
can.

And in your moment of truth
Yet just another day
The King will come and say "Well done"
And then be on his way

I am the king of In-Between, and right before your
eyes.
You'll never catch the likes of me, 'cause I know
how to hide.

And on and on you go
From each event you flow
"This moment"
Is your time to step beyond ... In-Between

Elements

Earth: Solid and true, steady to the touch
Mother remains herself

Fire: Fire purifies, not out of pain
But because fire burns through
That which is not you

Water: Peace is easy like a cool mountain stream
Yielding around rock formations
To keep moving

Air: Like the heart throb of a thunderstorm
The calm of a hurricane's eye
The colors of a sunset's splendor
Air remains ... unpredictably awesome

Mathias Karayan

No Man's Land

Caught in the middle, the edge of night
Something is moving, but I'm out of sight

Anticipating ... a friend or foe
It makes little difference, when it's my time I'll know

The lots cast before me, destinations all planned
Show me your answer, please if you can

Lost in the middle, alone in the dark
Projecting life's riddle, or igniting one's spark

Courage

In between dark and light
Are desires to fight

In between hot and cold
Are the thoughts that make me old

In between good and bad
Are days to feel sad

In between right and wrong
Are opportunities to sing a song

In between up and down
My feet are on the ground

In between fight or flight
My mind's drained of might

In between birth and death
I seek a moments rest

Mathias Karayan

In The Arms of God

Turbulent flows the mountain stream
Deep and dark its torrents
While subtle pools of sorrow gather
From its twisting current

I set my tent at valley's edge
From where the river flows
Above the pools of sorrow's gate
Lies the path I must go

I take my compass, water and food
To help me when it's time
My compass fails, my food turns stale
My water left behind

So I drink deep and long
From the torrents of my heart
Ever pushing through my fears
All I see is dark

Unexpected and unlooked for
Places of rest I find
Relief it is, temporarily
From the shadows of my mind

I cannot rest for long
In a place I feel alone
So I push on and on and on I go
Seeking shelter from my storm

Forgetting what I was looking for
I was totally lost it seemed
I found myself in the arms of God
Awoken from my fitful dream

Mathias Karayan

I Am You

I am the wind
Whispering through your mind
Winding through the dust of time

I am the ocean
Mysterious and deep
With secrets mine to keep

I am the mountain
Standing tall and true
With no easy way through

I am the river
Through you I start
Back to my heart

I am you

Beyond the Veil [196]

A realization is the experience of expansive release. It is recognition beyond the limits you have given your mind to experience. The body's senses are not a part of this experience.

In having psychic / intuitive experiences, do not underestimate the power of your mind to facilitate deception. Be aware of a desire to want to repeat these experiences. They are not something extra special.

There is no Secret Wisdom given only to a few. Wisdom may seem to be secret. But that would be to those who are unaware of it. Wisdom is not secret as much as you hide it from your view.

I asked and was told, "It is not for you to know." With defiance I stepped down to enter through a big wooden door representing where the Akasha records[197] were. I was denied access. The next instant I found myself as a spark of light darting around inside a caterpillar. The caterpillar dissipated . . . and I was pure light.

1985

---

[196] As stated in the prologue, the following experiences are the basis for this book.

[197] In theosophy and anthroposophy, the Akashic records are a collection of concise, detailed information of thoughts, events, and emotions believed by theosophists to be encoded in a non-physical plane of existence known as the etheric plane, or the library of ancient Wisdom.

Beware of the idea of a place of Wisdom outside of You. The Akasha records are within you. With this in mind, freely engage in your experiences as a means to move beyond them.

Vision Quest

Joseph Campbell quoting Black Elk: "*I saw myself on the central mountain of the world, the highest place, and I had a vision because I was seeing in the sacred manner of the world.*" The sacred mountain Campbell states was Harney Peak in South Dakota. And then Black Elk says, "*But the central mountain is everywhere.*"

There is a place in the outer world that meets the inner ... the place where movement and noise is stilled ... the place where the ever-changing meets the eternal ... the place where ... "You are the central mountain, and the central mountain is everywhere."[198]

---

[198] Joseph Campbell, The Power of Myth p89. When you experience "Having is Being," you are everything you need and you are everywhere.

Once Before

I saw her! It was the day before yesterday, the 20th of December.

She was simply parking her car, that's all. The setting sun touching her face ... caught me off guard. Her beautiful auburn hair ... such an earthly silhouette ... was outlining her now shining facial tones ... and the golden browns lit up her face. It overwhelmed me.

At that moment, I felt as if I was going through a whole autumn ... an autumn I had gone through with her, as if ... as if we met once before ... in another life.[199]

I was afraid to entertain this thought. But it was too late. I was taken by surprise. The thoughts and feelings that overwhelmed me I could not defend against. I looked again ...

In that moment she captured me ... and I loved it. I openly and unabashedly gazed at her.

I took this experience into my private world. Oh how unsettling this is.

12/22/85

---

[199] Past body recollection.

Mathias Karayan

All Are Called

I saw the moon (or was it the sun?) rising in my mind. From right to left it rose. As it arched out of the horizon it grew into a fiery red mass ... and then quickly settled into a well formed yellow circle.

When it reached its peak, it stopped and vibrated. Pulsating light waves radiated from its sphere like the ripples of a stone thrown into a clear calm lake.

Then it quickly shrunk back, into a white light ... beckoning me to come.[201]

I stepped forward ... but I could not make the journey. I could not yet take everyone with me.

1/21/86

---

[201] In some Hindu, Tao and Buddhist traditions, the third eye or mind's eye refers to the gate that leads to inner realms and spaces of higher consciousness. The concept of the third eye is a metaphor for non-dualistic thinking; the way the mystics see.

The Desert of Colorless Dreams[202]

I saw within me a hole ... a black center
Around that center was a desert ...
A desert of colorless dreams
There was no bush, no mountain, nothing around
me

... I saw nothingness ...
There was nothing to touch me
And I was perfectly safe

4/6/86

---

[202]"The Desert of Colorless Dreams" is a metaphorical phrase referring to a state of mind where aspirations and hopes have lost their vibrancy. It is a moment of having no need to seek, do or accomplish anything. In that moment, I understood the Tao of "Doing all without doing." I was at peace with myself and the world of nothingness around me.

Mathias Karayan

The Power of the Void

I touched the power of the void ...

    The chaos of the earth surrounded me as water swelled up and pounded the rocks around me. The splash of cold water kissed my brow as if to say "I am a friend ... but understand me. My kiss can kill those unaware ... those who take me for granted."

    I touched the power of the void ... as the mind tamed the body's senses ... senses which are part of the body ... a body which is part of the void.

Stand by your edge ...

    Feel the power of wind and waves crashing upon the rocks around you. Embrace this power ... take it in ... feel it ... let it flow through you ... let it shake your very foundation to the bone. Let it tempt you with its overpowering despair.

Step into the void ...

    Feel the void of power as the body's senses recoil in its fearful lick of death swelling and crashing within you. Here ... in the void of power ... you will find the gentle repose of peaceful Being.

On the shore of Lake Superior
6/21/86

Merging with the Light

Surrounded by darkness, as if in midair, I reached up to open a door. As the door slowly cracked open, white light spread out around its edges. I stepped forward and walked in. For just an instant, to my surprise, and yet not ... I met myself at the door.

203

---

[203] Drawing by Rachael Balsaitis

As my eyes became accustomed to the bright light, I recognized everyone I would think of in this joyful atmosphere. Some had already transitioned from the body. Some were currently projecting a body on earth. In this place, all had transparent bodies.

Some came up to me and said with a smile, "I see you made it the hard way ... while you're still living with a body on earth." They would plead, "Please talk to me when you get back to earth! I want to wake up!"

I responded, "I will, yes I will, I won't forget!"[204] I heard myself thinking this in unison with whoever was pleading with me ... so I wouldn't forget this place ... so I would also remember to awaken.

Then a still small voice said "Please listen."

11/17/87

---

[204] These conversations were all experienced without spoken words.

Beyond the Horizon of Light

Hidden in the shadow of the dark side of a planet, I effortlessly sped along above the surface.[205] Hugging the planet's dark surface, I moved towards the horizon of light. The horizon gradually became a dark red, changing quickly to a bright molten red.

Suddenly, the ground fell away as I shot out over the molten yellow red horizon of the planet. Looking below, I was overwhelmed by wind driven swirls of yellow white gaseous fire. The wind driven swirls moved across what seemed an expansive ocean planet of turbulent liquid gas and fire.

Immediately I realized ... I was looking directly into the sun over Mercury's horizon. It was a calm day. I noticed no need to protect my eyes from the light, nor my face from the heat.

3/5/88

---

[205] Astral projection. An out of body experience is not really an out of body experience as much as it is a recognition of you, being *other than* a body.

I Met Him

I stood about 20 feet away and slightly downhill ... looking up at this huge stone altar. The altar was about ten feet square and about eight feet high. On the altar was the burning of an animal; an animal sacrifice. I was not able to see the sacrifice that was burning. Off of the top of this altar rolled a curling thick smoke.

"There's got to be a better way to know God than this" I thought. At that moment, around the corner to my right walked Jesus. I recognized him immediately. Swiftly he walked by ... between myself and the altar. A small caravan of people were hustling to catch up.

In the next instant I was looking out upon a crowd over Jesus' right shoulder as he sat above them on a hillside.[206]

1990

[206] Past body recollection.

Wake Up!

As I was sleeping on my back, I woke up to a rattling sound. I thought someone was trying to break into the house. I tried to get up but could not move. I tried to speak but could not warn my wife. No matter how hard I tried, I was paralyzed. I was terrified.

Then I saw the form of a face slowly appear looking over me as I lay on my back. The face unknown to me, was composed of white smoke. I did not recognize it. It was scary to me. The smoke changed to make other faces. I blew at it and it dissipated.

Then I woke up from the dream I thought I had already awoken from … and a still small voice said to me "Wake up!" ... as if I was still sleeping.[207]

1/22/07

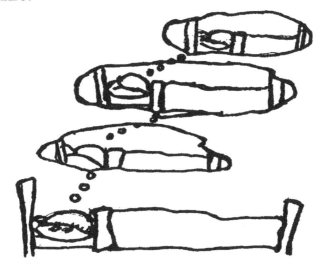

---

[207] A visitation.

Appendix

Women of the Moon

Preface

In the dream ... anything is possible
When you awaken ... possibility is irrelevant
In the meantime ... welcome to the dream[208]

Introduction

There is an ancient hate ... so ancient, its reason has been long forgotten. Even so, this ancient hate still plays out in our daily relationships through anger, guilt and fear.

There is also a love more ancient than this hate. Though also forgotten as to its source, it is a love that transcends this hate because it is a love we all share ...

---

[208] Spirit does not know of time. If you believe in time, you deny your reality in spirit. This is called dreaming. Remember, this story is within the context of a dream of awakening. Therefore, beyond the dream this story does not exist.

and this we share because we all share the same Source. Here is where our story begins ... in the same place as its ending.

It was within a thought of lunacy that the inception of Og-dog took hold ....
  And in the dark did He reign

* * *

  From out of darkness came a call for help ...
And from out of the Dawn came an answer.

Mathias Karayan

Let the celestial rays of light
Reflected in the night
Give way to sight
Beheld in the Inner Light

* * *

Listen people far and near
Of times forgotten, now many years
"Just stories" some say "children's tales"
Yet truth to those whose hearts don't fail

With sweat and tears we turn the soil
Shedding blood, the curse of toil
The darkest hour that rules the night
Must give way to the dawning light[209]

---

[209] All excerpts from The Archives of Pythia (one among the descended children of light), except where otherwise noted. Pythia was the recorder for the task of this particular community of light. Over the centuries in ancient Greek mythology, Pythia became the name of the High Priestess of the Temple of Apollo at Delphi who also served as the oracle, commonly known as the Oracle of Delphi. Pythia maintained a strong connection with the other side of the veil.

The Last Stand

Atlantis: The last stand before the turning away from the Source of light ... for the darkness of an ephemeral body.[210]

The Information Age

Once upon a time, a long time ago, during the decline of the Atlantean Golden Age, an influx of information surfaced. The information was overwhelming and alluring. It was hope to many of that day that reform would bring them back to the fading remembrance of "The Golden Age of Reason." Possibilities seemed limitless. Because information flourished they coined this period of their history, "The Information Age."

From where this information came, and the details of how it was given, is another topic of conversation.[211] It is enough to say "you had not yet mastered an understanding of your physical bodies as we had hoped."

Knowledge was given anticipating it would speed you along. But those who gave the knowledge were

---

[210] Short lived, transient, fleeting, momentary, brief, temporary. The making of reincarnation.

[211] As expressed through The Lost Annals of Atlantis.

not aware of the seduction of the ephemeral. Instead of using it for the understanding and mastering of your body, you used it to placate it. This lostness into the seduction of the ephemeral precipitated a plan for correction. However, this plan for correction would come with the cost of a bitter twist

The Community of Light

It all began when some descendants of light wandered off into idol thinking ... becoming bewildered spirits.

As bewildered, they became vulnerable to the temptation, the allure of the ephemeral. Through this alluring intoxication, they gave up the memory of a transparent self to wander into the density of ephemeral bodies.

Symbols of Power in Metaphysics

Through an influx of information, the bewildered descendants had risen to a civilized level of consciousness. This was the dawning of earth's civilization, its first golden age. Being the closest in time to the memory of its own Light, it could be considered the greatest age of earth's civilizations.

The idle chatter of our age has glorified that age with an exaggeration that the Atlanteans were particularly enlightened. True, it was advanced for a community beginning to realize its spiritual potential. However, it was only a dawning. "You had not yet mastered your ephemeral vehicle. The central truths that re-introduced you to an awareness above animal instinct were being taken for granted. Few among you could see your growing complacency through an expanding ocean of dis-information."[212] Complacency came in the form of rituals and incantations around their identity of a dense body image.

As the community of light started to wane in an ocean of information, darkness slowly encroached. Information overload impaired the Atlanteans ability to read the signs of this subtle intrusion. Nor did they

---

[212] How different is this from a computer chip jam packed with the information of our day? Information misused is just what it is ... ink on paper.

take seriously a growing magnitude of earth tremors that warned of an approaching global shift.

A flood of fire, volcanic ash and title waves of water caused by an earth shift sent the civilization into exile.[213] Their complacency prevented their escape from the allure of the ephemeral.

---

[213] "The Wave" was painted by Whispering Star of the mid-atlantean period and hung in the Tower of Light for 500 years. Whispering Star was one of the seven sisters of the Pleiades. As expressed through The Lost Annals of Atlantis.

The Plan

Just prior to the Atlanteans dispersion into exile, came a call for help received at dawn's gate. To avoid a setback into darkness a plan was carefully conceived to raise the community out of confusion. Contact would have to be made. The time of most significant contact remained the elusive variable in the successful carrying out of the plan.

The earth's next global shake down was to be the window of opportunity for the children out of the dawn to redirect the lost children out of darkness. To misjudge this time would be the delay of the plan's fulfillment with the ushering in of the age of Og-dog's reign on earth. This reign would end with the earth's destruction. It would be a desolate and dark planet. Yet hope's call for help was given an answer by the promise of a plan.

Mathias Karayan

From out of darkness a light shines
To guide the many, the children of our time
Truth their witness, the witness from the Old
Anchored in remembrance, the story will be told [214]

Contact would be made by entities of light. These children of light arriving out of the dawn would have to interface directly with darkness through an ephemeral vehicle. As bearers of light they would use astral mobility as a buffer to touch the ephemeral without risking undo exposure to its entanglement. With an astral infusion strong enough to facilitate a global rising of consciousness, they could thwart the encroachment of darkness.

Those out of the dawn knew the risk involved. Astral mobility was their link to return to the celestial realm at their appointed time. To lose astral grounding for the intoxicating allure of "a self" in the ephemeral would be to wander in the kingdom of darkness for an undetermined time. Remaining grounded in the astral was a matter of grave importance.

---

[214] As expressed through The Archives of Pythia.

A Falling Out

As stewards of the Kingdom of Light, a discreet group left the celestial order out of the dawn to encounter the ephemeral realm of consciousness. Contact conceived to coincide with a global speed-up was in progress.

To the surprise of the children of light, the many were not willing to rise to the occasion. The distraction of an earlier influx of "information" left the Atlanteans indifferent, distracted, know it all's and stubborn. Prolonged exposure into the beguiling and alluring nature of the ephemeral by the children of light in a last ditch attempt to turn the tide, proved disastrous. The plan went awry with a falling out within the group by the misuse of power. Some found their use of "special abilities" in the ephemeral a temptation of power that they were not able to resist. The rest is history.

> *Woman with a weapon*
> *So fearsome to behold*
> *Your teeth strong as iron*
> *Your heart cold as snow*[215]

---

[215] All excerpts expressed through the minstrel Parnassus (one among the descended children of light), are through

Some among the group discharged themselves from their appointed task. They walked into the darkness of the ephemeral to practice the arts known to them from the astral realm. In the realm of Og-dog they would eventually be twisted by deceit for personal gain.

> *You stalk your prey with relish*
> *To another's despair*
> *Your weaving dreams are hellish*
> *But oh you seem so fair* [216]

To this day, the confusion of lostness is strong among those who have misused a healing power for personal gain.

> *When you gonna' wake up*
> *And look at what you hold*
> *Don't you ever wonder*
> *About the birthright you sold?* [217]

The Archives of Pythia. Mount Parnassus is a sacred mountain in central Greece, near Delphi. The name "Parnassus" in literature typically refers to its distinction as the home of poetry, literature and learning.

[216] Ibid

[217] Ibid

They forsook their grounding in the astral for a home in the ephemeral. Their responsibility to return remains the strongest within their own inner conflict.

The Great Council [218]

With the Eastern sun rose Wisdom
And in its Western sky shall both reign

After the group's falling out the remaining found themselves in a dilemma. That which was started as an opportunity for speed-up, appeared as a stumbling block to healing. The conversation among the remaining children was tense. Sophia,[219] the orders leader, calls a council with those left in the group.

"Oh my" begins a shaken Sophia through natural mind communication.[220] "What have we done?! Not

---

[218] The dialogue of The Great Council, expressed through The Archives of Pythia.

[219] The Ancient Greek word Sophia is the abstract noun of σοφός which variously translates as "clever, skillful, intelligent and wise".

[220] Communication was naturally non-verbal. Out of necessity of living as separated identities on earth, they

only do we find ourselves in a wicked time, we are also its participants!"

"What are we to do?" exclaims Parvati[221] doubtfully, "our appointed time of return draws nigh!"

For a brief moment the council engaged in confusion. Confusion and doubt were experiences new to them. So was the feeling of panic. The ephemeral was having an effect.

As if to break the enchantment of a subtle slumber, Gabriella flared,[222] "In the name of light, am I not responsible to face my departed kindred?!" All eyes focused on Gabriella. "I must remain resolute in following through with the plan. I know ..." hesitated Gabriella, "I know I shall have to become mortal."

---

learned to imitate verbal communication. As their remembrances faded through the body life cycles of time, mind communication became the exception. This potential still remains, to be used at the given time.

[221] Parvati is the Hindu goddess of fertility, love and devotion; as well as of divine strength and power. She is the mythical daughter of King Himalaya; after the Hindu tradition.

[222] Gabriella's appearance was to be the inspiration for the traditional stories of the angel Gabriel, the messenger of Light.

Symbols of Power in Metaphysics

The floor of the council became hushed. All knew what the personal cost would be to wander through the ephemeral ... for an unknown amount of time.

Finally, breaking the silence, Pericles[223] tested Gabriella's resolve with a verbal affront, "Are you sure you know what you are saying, Gabriella?"

"Why do you ask?" Gabriella contended verbally, "do we not share the same Mind?!"

Rising to stand with Gabriella, Phoebe[224] spoke, "I too shall walk with Gabriella as a light into the darkness."

Shadows out of darkness
With the setting of the sun
Is you Moon Child
A light to everyone[225]

---

[223] Under the leadership of Pericles (reincarnated 495-429 B.C.), the golden age of Athenian culture flourished. Pericles was a brilliant general, orator, patron of the arts and politician; "the first citizen" of democratic Athens, according to the historian Thucydides.

[224] Phoebe is found in Greek mythology, sometimes associated as the goddess of the moon. In poetry, Phoebe is the moon personified.

[225] As expressed through the minstrel Parnassus.

It would take a desperate plan to counter desperate times.

It was decided that a representation would depart in the name of light to offset the defection that had occurred. They knew if they crossed over into the ephemeral realm as mortal beings their journey back would be carried through the repetition of many body life experiences.

Time is an encounter that finds you in a body image[226]

They also knew they would eventually lose their natural awareness of astral mobility. To lose this awareness would be to lose any guarantee of the time of return to the celestial. But they also knew the plan was a promise that would be fulfilled ... in time.

Contact

*Through a corridor of space we quickly flew
Into a portal of time we quietly slipped through*[227]

---

[226] As expressed through The Archives of Pythia.
[227] Ibid

Symbols of Power in Metaphysics

To the many of that time, an unusual esoteric order [228]appeared suddenly and apparently, from out of nowhere. Besides their sudden appearance, this order was considered unusual in their practice of the creative arts and sciences. Not only were they discerning regarding the signs of the time through the stars of the sky, they also exhibited an unusual skill in the mastering of their ephemeral vehicle.

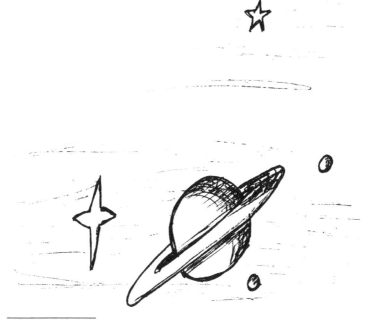

---

[228] This group as human spirits for a time, will forget they are divine beings, not remembering how to escape from the ephemeral. It is their task to acquire the knowledge and tools needed in order to be free of the body and return to their purely spiritual home.

The Lost Annals of Atlantis[229] mention the appearance of an "extraordinary" group of women who seemed to have a "magical" quality about them. Also, because of their skill in the arts of healing, many through their own twisted religious fears sought them out to persecute and kill them.

Because their appearance coincided with a lunar shift that reflected a surprisingly dramatic increase of light into the night, this order became known by the many of that time as Women of the Moon. Pythia was the order's historian and appointed recorder. The Archives of Pythia provides accurate accounts of the triumphs and tragedies of that time.

The order's sudden appearance from beyond the experience of the ephemeral was an indication of their proficiency in astral mobility. The Atlanteans already possessed passed down information regarding astral mobility. Their lack of personal grounding and focus prevented them from practicing it. As Sophia expresses in The Archives of Pythia. "We knew

---

[229] Contrary to popular opinion, the Atlanteans passed down written symbols. Much of the information from this source regarding this order was passed down through misunderstandings that exaggerate encounters into irrelevant or weird folklore.

information grazers would attempt to manipulate natural mobility as a magical power. That is why they were lost in their own magical thinking." Sophia understood that the Atlanteans already demonstrated a vulnerability to misuse natural abilities.

The Dispersion

As a safeguard against the seduction of the ephemeral, and knowing that the many would misinterpret their abilities in fearful ways, the order remained clandestine.

The order's understanding of natural earth medicine enabled them to maintain an ephemeral vehicle well over three hundred years.

Some lived long enough to witness the great dispersion of the Atlanteans. For them it was the dispersion of their light into the darkness. Whispering Star, painter of the impending flood on the Great Hall of Justice was one among the last remaining order, who lived to see its prophecy fulfilled. Gaia,[230] the most adept in natural earth medicine maintained her initial ephemeral body vehicle for well over five hundred earth cycles. Pythia, also remained with her ephemeral body as one of the last of the original descended.

---

[230] Through Greek mythology, Gaia became larger than life as the first Greek god, or actually goddess. According to Greek mythology, Gaia, or Mother Earth, created herself out of primordial chaos. From her fertile womb all life sprang, and unto Mother Earth all living things must return after their allotted span of life is over.

Symbols of Power in Metaphysics

Through the changing of the seasons
The autumn of your despair
The change will never catch you
Moon Child oh so fair [231]

Continuity

As the first of the stewardship during the kingdom's exile, these Women of The Moon were a haven of light through the onset of the storm. Their work during their initial appearance was to pass the torch ... and then in their separate ways fade into the reincarnation of human history. Their passing of the torch was the surety of continuity that would ignite the ages to come. As mortal with special abilities, they mingled with and became subjected to the cycle of birth to death to birth. Because of the promise, their lineage of consciousness has endured the prolonged storm of darkness. Continuing to work behind the scenes to complete their mission, they have made periodic corrective appearances throughout earth history. Because the seduction of information has an alluring effect on the mind given over to an ephemeral body, some forgetfulness has occurred over time.

---

[231] As expressed through the minstrel Parnassus.

Lord of Love, Lord of Light
Guide us through this moonless night
Will we wander and wonder why
Where You are to catch our eye
Take our hands, guide our thoughts
Help us see what we forgot

Lord of Love, Lord of Light
Guide us through this moonless night
Give us a reason, give us a rhyme
To dance together till the end of time[232]

"This chant, passed down within the order, bound us to remain on task. We knew our journey back would be a long one tied to the course and culmination of human history. The greater our initial strength together, the stronger the lineage's extension over the reincarnation of time. The stronger our extension, the greater our influence over the course of human history. Those who became waylaid over time would decrease the strength of our inherent cohesion to influence correction. Initiates introduced into the lineage would

---

[232] As expressed through The Archives of Pythia.

provide renewed strength to carry us through the course of influencing human history."[233]

Those who survived beyond the forgetfulness of the dispersion did so through their writings or the writings of others about them. Sappho,[234] Mary Magdalene the partner of Jesus, Murasaki Shikibu, Sacajawea, Harriet Tubman, Helena Blavatsky, Alice Bailey, Mary Baker Eddy, Saint Thérèse of Lisieux and Mother Theresa are a few notable descendants reappearing throughout history. On The Great Day of Recognition those who labored to keep the course of human history on task will be remembered and honored for their labor of love.

The Return

---

[233] Ibid

[234] There is little known about Sappho (630-570BC) except that she was an Archaic Greek poet from Eresos or Mytilene on the island of Lesbos. Sappho is known for her lyric poetry of love, written to be sung while accompanied by music. In ancient times, Sappho was widely regarded as one of the greatest lyric poets and was given names such as the "Tenth Muse" and "The Poetess." Most of Sappho's poetry is now lost. She is the reincarnated Parnassus.

Over the past two hundred years an explosion of women of distinction have emerged to greatly influence the direction of earth history. They are not a result of growing male tolerance and awareness. They are a cause of it. This cause is also working in conjunction with others towards the accomplishment of a greater plan. The race to meet mother earth at her next time of global speed-up is drawing nigh.

The order's initial task to offset the defection is near completion. When the next juncture for global speed-up presents itself, the children of light who did not descend into the ephemeral realm will return to the astral realm. They will work to awaken all who descended from the council. Those who await their arrival look to the sky for the signs of their coming.

Some say that even now, in this day and age, children of light are selectively contacting their kindred on earth. That which may appear as an "angelic" encounter to some is actually a reconnection of a child of light out of the astral. This does not mean the encounter is not angelic.

This explosion over the last two hundred years is an indication of the nearness of the next major global speed-up. Although a lifestyle change will be required, that is only an effect of an inner psychic change.

"Just as in the days of the 'free thinking' Atlanteans, your opportunity for a mental shift is nearing. You are being prepared to rise to the occasion of Mother Earth's shift. Due to the fact that you seem unable to make noticeable progress on your own, you will be given a push. Individually, it will manifest as out of control conflict. It is a push for resolution to higher ground. Globally, a planetary shift will pull you into a crash / burn course (like the Atlanteans). It can also be used as a sling to propel you beyond your resistance to shift. Your current lifestyle will not endure. You will have to get your mind out of the way so you can once again understand balance through the song of a bird and feel the heartbeat of a tree."[235]

------

[235] As expressed by Sophia through The Archives of Pythia.

What about the Defection?

> *The mountain tops your crown babe*
> *The deep brown earth your throne*
> *When you gonna' wake up*
> *And start the journey home[236]*

Those who were allured from astral grounding in the name of ephemeral power became diluted by darkness. However,

> *The earth is but a dream*
> *It's never as it seems[237]*

Before the dawn, all willingly choose to serve light. There is no spell the dark lord, Og-dog, can conjure up that will break a contract established before the dawn. However, because of those who defected from the Great Council, discharging themselves from their appointed task into the allure and lostness of darkness, they will need tremendous help to awaken.

> *How long shall Og-dog's nightmare reign*
> *In the hearts and minds of mortal kind?[238]*

---

[236] As expressed through the minstrel Parnassus.

[237] Ibid

[238] As expressed through The Archives of Pythia.

Symbols of Power in Metaphysics

Out of love did all children out of the dawn answer the call for help. Through loves answer, they were sealed by a promise. Love's promise is that none of the departed kindred would be lost forever. The Kingdom of Light would be made manifest to once again reign in the hearts of all children who wandered into darkness.

> *Your feet are planted firmly*
> *You have your celestial journey*
> *A new name I bequeath you*
> *Moon Child of Elysium*[239]

Those who left astral grounding for the ephemeral in the name of light and love to thwart the initial infiltration of their fallen kindred, have one more part to play. They will finish what they came to do. They will face the departed kindred.

> *Shadows out of darkness*
> *With the setting of the sun*
> *Is you Moon Child*
> *A light to everyone*[240]

---

[239] As expressed through the minstrel Parnassus.

[240] Ibid

What the moon represents

Because the moon is ephemeral in nature, its deception is its reflection ... unless you recognize its metaphorical nature for what it is, a mirror for the light to enter your darkness.

The new moon represents unity, resolve, focus and repose. The full moon represents independence, polarity, the dispersion of reflected light. Both serve a purpose.

During the time of Og-dog's domination through darkness, the Women of The Moon drew their own light through inner reflection, celebrated as the full moon shedding light into the shadow of Og-dog's darkness. This inner reflection served as a unifying force for the order that thwarted lunar polarity. Lunar polarity is a distraction to the ephemeral body (lunacy). Through their own inner light, darkness could not touch them. It was their centering, meditative resolve that provided them the strength to endure the ephemeral lure over many life times.

Symbols of Power in Metaphysics

Without opening your door
You can open your heart to the world
Without looking out your window
You can see the essence of the Way[241]

The full moon represented polarity, conflict. Yet, as an asset it assisted in their memory of astral mobility. This assistance protected them from the seduction of the ephemeral. Through their own polarity they refused to adjust and find a place of rest in Og-dog's domain. Instead, they shined as beacons in a lighthouse in the shadows of a great storm. Their work of love robbed Og-dog of complete domination. The moon's light reflected on the dark side of earth demonstrated the promise for all to see.

---

[241] Lao-tzu, Tao Te Ching #47. Nothing is known about Lao-tzu. In one account, Sima Qian (145–86 BC), a Chinese historian of the early Han dynasty, reports that Laozi or Lao-tzu was said to be a contemporary of Confucius during the 6th or 5th century BC. Although the Tao Te Ching by some, is attributed to a number of authors, it is more likely that because of the internal consistency of the book that Lao-tzu was the author. The teachings of Lao-tzu is by far the most female of all the great world religions. Lao-tzu is the reincarnation of Sophia.

Mathias Karayan

In the time of darkness, Og-dog's domain
A full moon rises, to rob Og-dog's reign[242]

Total absorption into darkness was repulsed by polarity. The dream of darkness could not overwhelm everyone.

To this day, the full moon represents a reminder of this order's polarity (conflict) in time and space (the ephemeral). Sensitivity to lunar polarity has a sobering effect of tension on the ephemeral vehicle. It reminds this order to differentiate between what is true and what is an imagination of shadows within the ephemeral tug of war. As divine beings within this internal tug of war, they could not find the comfort to make the ephemeral their home. As the minstrel Parnassus once sang;

> *Child of the Moon*
> *Woman of the sea*
> *Between ebb and flow*
> *Waiting restlessly*

Og-dog could not hide from the moon. The Children of the Promise who did not discharge their

---

[242] As expressed through The Archives of Pythia.

duties for the allure of ephemeral darkness could expose the darkness by reflecting light. But they could not resolve their own tension of ephemeral polarity. They are locked in a struggle for balance between the astral realm of consciousness and the ephemeral realm of consciousness. To come from (or be grounded in) the astral and lost to the ephemeral is a battle ground. There is no place to rest except in the promise. Their conflict (polarity) is between realms of consciousness. In short, how do you live in a place of peace in your mind that is not your home?

Children of the Promise

> *Children of the Promise*
> *You will know who*
> *What I say here*
> *Is written just for you*[243]

Today's Children of the Promise, journey to remember their heritage. Polarity, or the reflection of light from beyond is your reminder of the work you need to do for resolution. It is the irritation of a piece of sand that makes the pearl. It is the conflict between

---

[243] As expressed through The Archives of Pythia.

realms of consciousness that is arousing those who came back for the departed brethren.

The departed brethren who discharged their duties for the allure of ephemeral darkness, struggle between light and darkness. For they used their skills as light workers to be twisted in Og-dog's darkness.

> *Will you find your empty dreams*
> *Among the broken pottage*
> *Or look beyond your plastic schemes*
> *To your home bound cottage*[244]

For both, it is a call to awareness; to begin communication and yielding for your appointed rendezvous. Within the greater plan of speed-up you must shift to learn repose.

For the departed brethren, lost in the darkness, their shift is a transfer to unite with the "new" moon. It is a practicing to re-frame the darkness as a way to bring in personal light. There is a transcendence in experiencing the new as the full, as the full is the new.

As Sophia states through The Archives of Pythia, "You must unlearn independence in the name of mutual interdependence. Your most immediate task

---

[244] As expressed through the minstrel Parnassus.

is intrapsychic, to work for resolution, for one minded grounding. You cannot move on until this matter is resolved. Again, your conflict is not between realms of consciousness. It is between light and darkness. How do you transform the darkness you got lost in for light?"

In the name of darkness, the departed renounced their grounding. Their lostness to the ephemeral is strong. Their work will be one of renunciation. They will have to abandon everything they have invested in as their personal ground of power before they can move on to the re-dedication of light. It will involve concentration of focus, adjustment and courage ... unless they take the short cut ... through the humility of redirection.

In growing awareness do all children of the promise celebrate the fullness of the moon. That is, while the full reminds you of light from outside, the new reminds you of the light you are from within. This balance is your window of greatest opportunity. It is the place to transcend polarity for your remembrance of singularity.

Clarification

All children of light are gender-less. Before the dawn, the Ancient's will tell you "all that is, is One." The descended order chose the feminine persuasion of the ephemeral at a time most beneficial for the long term accomplishment of a plan gone astray. A particular gender identity was not to be an end in itself. They did not descend to become women. They arrived to complete a mission gone awry. Throughout the ages, most have held strong to the gender of their original incarnation out of a sense of familiarity. They are moving beyond the polarity of gender identification.

The returning children out of the dawn will not be looking to reconnect with "Women" of the Moon. They will be looking for the heart of a child of light. Gender identity in the ephemeral can be used as a cloak of elitism, self-deception. The spark of a child of light cannot be hidden from those who look with vision. Those out of the dawn are not invested through eyes of the ephemeral. "It is not unlikely in our day to find some among us inhabiting male bodies in order to further the plan."

The Gates of Remembrance

Today's Children of the Promise are heirs on the cusp of an age waiting for their awakening. Infatuation with the dusk and dawn, the moon, and the stars are strong indications of their stirring. Just as a desert rain at night gives way to a morning blanket of fragrantly colorful spring flowers, so too will their stark and unusual awakening be when they lead the lost kindred into the age of light.

The rain must come to pass
So the promise made is realized at last[245]

When all children of the original plan meet again at the gates of Elysium,[246] there will be tears of joy and celebration of laughter like none witnessed out of the

---

[245] As expressed through The Archives of Pythia.

[246] Elysium or the Elysian Fields is a conception of the afterlife that developed over time and was maintained by some Greek religious and philosophical sects.

dawn. They have all finally returned to The Gates of Remembrance, at dawn's break.

"I Pythia, one among the descended children of light, bear witness to the events of light and love expressed through the work of the kinship. I say this to prepare you for the plan's realization and the promise of return. In the name of this remembrance is the story told."

Let the celestial rays of light, reflected in the night
Give way to sight, beheld in the Inner Light

Moon Child of Elysium[247]

Verse:

> Shadows out of darkness
> With the setting of the sun
> Is you Moon Child
> A light to everyone
> Through the changing of the seasons
> The autumn of your despair
> The change will never catch you
> Moon Child oh so fair

Chorus:

> The earth is but a dream
> It's never as it seems
> Your feet are planted firmly
> You have your celestial journey
> A new name I bequeath you
> Moon Child of Elysium

---

[247] As expressed through the minstrel Parnassus.

Mathias Karayan

Verse:

> Child of the Moon
> Woman of the sea
> Between ebb and flow
> Waiting restlessly
> Through the changing of the seasons
> The autumn of your despair
> The change will never catch you
> Moon Child oh so fair

Chorus:

> The sun reflects your splendor
> The aura of the Moon
> Your feet are planted firmly
> You have your celestial journey
> A new name I bequeath you
> Moon Child of Elysium

Symbols of Power in Metaphysics

Woman with a Weapon[248]

Verse:

> Woman with a weapon
> So fearsome to behold
> Your teeth strong as iron
> Your heart cold as snow
>
> You stock your prey with relish
> To another one's despair
> Your weaving dreams are hellish
> But oh you seem so fair

Chorus:

> When you gonna' wake up
> And look at what you hold
> Or don't you ever wonder
> About the birthright you sold

---

[248] As expressed through the minstrel Parnassus.

Mathias Karayan

Verse:

> You calculate your future
> Precision beyond compare
> Plot your every movement
> With mi-nute care

> Hoping for the right one
> A pauper or a king
> Cast your spell among us
> Keep us all dancing

Chorus:

> Will you find your empty dreams?
> Among the broken pottage
> Or look beyond your plastic schemes
> To your home bound cottage

Verse:

> The mountain tops your crown babe
> The deep brown earth your throne
> When you gonna' wake up
> And start your journey home

Symbols of Power in Metaphysics

Verse:

> Woman with a weapon
> So fearsome to behold
> Your teeth strong as iron
> Your heart oh so cold

Mathias Karayan

Clarification of Relationship

New Moon: This is the phase of the moon moving between the earth and the sun. With the moon aligned with the will of the sun, flow is in on direction, to the sun. In relation to the earth's position, the alignment is of maximal effect for unifying (centering) energy. This is also known as the period of repose (rest). When the earth becomes a backdrop for the moon to cast its shadow, the alignment is called a solar eclipse. This is the will of three, approaching maximal alignment.

Full Moon: This is when the earth moves between the moon and sun. There is a pull of two wills from opposite directions. Energy flow, if unprotected is pulled apart, polarized, divided, diffused, rather than united and empowering. During a full moon phase, oneness of purpose and focus is important. Not only is there the greatest opportunity for creativity, but also for irritation, agitation, restlessness (lunacy). This is when the sun reflects its glory on the the moon, shining its light on the dark side of the earth. This is the metaphor for letting the light into the dark corners of your mind.

Symbols of Power in Metaphysics

When the moon becomes a backdrop for the earth to cast its shadow, the alignment is called a lunar eclipse. The will of the earth is in a phase of maximal polarity.

Half Moon: The first and third quarter moon is in a triangular relationship with the earth and sun. This represents balance. Not only is there a pulling apart, there is unifying effect. This balance (cancellation) of opposing effects is in-between the emergence of the moon's next phase, which is either ephemeral tension or astral repose.

A Celebration of Light

A practice within the kinship for the remembrance of the Promise to be fulfilled.

As you allow a chosen one to bring a lit candle into a dark room, that one says "This light represents The Light of Love entering from the Dawn."

As this chosen one lights the candle held in the first recipients right hand, this first recipient says for all; "From out of the darkness, from beyond the ephemeral realm, do we receive light ... The light of ourselves ... the light of love."

The first recipient crosses their heart by the reaching over to light another's candle on their left. As they light the candle to their left they state "This light of myself do I pass to another ... the light of love."

As each participant passes on the light from right to left, one to another they say "This light of myself do I pass to another ... the light of love."

Ending ceremony / Renewed pledge

At the end of the passing of light, the group in a unifying resolve, reminded of their original task,[249] say

---

[249] Remember, your original task is to shine your light into the darkness. This you do by the practice of forgiveness.

as a whole, "My only function here is to share healing. I do not need to know what that means, or how it looks. I just need to be willing to practice it wherever I go. For the time I am given to complete my task is the time I will use as a way back out of time . . . to my awakening in the Dawn." So;

Shine your light, so I can see
Your smiling face, looking back at me.
Shine your light, so I can see
The path that leads between ... you and me

Matt Karayan
Shine Your Light

Glossary

The Astral Realm – Because you project a body image into space and time, you can also project an astral or light body image into the ethereal plane of experience. Without the limits of a material body, you have a mobility of movement through space as an ethereal identity.

Collapse of Time – Time was made as the time you need to undo the original error. Time is shortened between you and your memory of eternity when a particular lesson is learned through forgiveness. This lesson learned is an experience beyond the senses of the ephemeral called by names such as epiphanies, miracles, spiritual realizations, etc. The illusion of time seems to collapse when there is one less substitution (limiting symbol of belief) between you and your memory of Source. Also referred to as a **speed-up.**

Déjà Vu – A Déjà Vu experience is a fleeting remembrance of a past body experience triggered by a present stimulus encounter. It is as if "I've lived this moment before, exactly as it's happening now." It's like a memory and a moment in one. As you try to savor the experience, it fades. Now only its fleeting memory remains.

Dreaming – Spirit does not know of time and space. If you believe in time and space you deny your reality in Spirit. This is called dreaming.

Ephemeral – Movement and noise as fleeting, momentary, transient, temporary, passing, brief, short-lived, etc. In other words, life as experienced through a body.

Ethereal plane – Other than the physical plane, and just on the other side of the veil, the ethereal plane is a subtle state of consciousness that transcends the known physical universe. It is experienced apart from the five senses.

Forgiveness as Real – Properly understood, real forgiveness recognizes that error is merely a mistaken perception needing correction at the level of your mind, not in the projection of mind's error called the world. That separate minds and bodies clash is a given. However, real forgiveness recognizes that what you thought another did to you or what you did to another was a mistake in interpretation. Out of ignorance or confusion, individual thoughts projected through bodies, clash. Real forgiveness asks "What do you want to make it mean?" To see beyond the immediate of taking it personally is a view that forgives your fixed perception of what you once made it mean in a self hurtful way. This is the undoing of karma and your collapse of time bringing you closer to your awakening from your dream of nothingness.

From this point of view, the only function meaningful in time is forgiveness. At your door to eternity you realize that the last illusion was that there was nothing to forgive. In the meantime you do the work of forgiving. In other words, and though you do not always realize it, the gift you give to anyone is the gift you always give to yourself first.

Healed Healer – The healed healer understands what part real forgiveness plays in their own journey towards waking up. Rather than being caught up in the conflicts and issues of the ever-changing spin, the healed healer stands as a light beyond the dream.

Healing – If sickness is mind's attempt to limit itself to something it is not, healing would be a changed mind about this belief, always experienced as release, not relief.

Idol – Any person, place or thing you invest in for happiness is an idol.[250] You know it is an idol when it also appears to make you unhappy. Your unhappiness is an example of a poor investment, an investment in something that is transient in nature, outside of You. It is not the idol that has made you unhappy. It is your investment in it as a Symbol of Power that makes you unhappy. Lasting relationships are not between bodies. They are of the Spirit. When fond memories do not involve emotional pain, you meet them in spirit.

Karma as Instant – Because "no thought leaves its source," how you view another or another's behavior, always affects you first. This is the making of your karma as instant. In other words, to justify "hating" someone for how you perceive what they did to you is to experience hate in your mind the instant you think it. Now you carry the karma of self attack to be undone at another time. To see another's struggle as your own, is a forgiving view.

[250] This is also the definition for co-dependency. *Transformational Psychotherapy P234-252*

It is not forgiving another for what you perceived they did to you. It is forgiving yourself for perceiving another in a way that you attacked your peace of mind. Because time was made to undo your karma, to forgive your karma (or to see it differently) is to experience your epiphany, speed-up or collapse of time. It's the work that undoes your need to reincarnate. And though you do not always realize it, the gift you give to anyone is the gift you always give to yourself first.

Karma over time is the unconscious memories you carry from one body experience to the next as pleasurable or painful, good or bad. They are interpretations held onto as personally real.

Mind over Matter – Mind over matter is true. You do not the experience mind over matter consistently because your mind is so out of control that you have depreciated the limitless value of its power. Mind over matter and "thinking positive" are two different things. Your projection of a self as a body image is mind over matter in denial that you did it. Thinking positive about nothingness is your attempt to make the ephemeral real. It has no value towards your journey to wake up. Rather, you need to do the work that forgiveness offers.

Miracle – It is the experience of your mind freed of its limiting beliefs through forgiveness. This is release, not relief. Relief is the experience of rearranging the temporary or modifying your thinking to spiritualize the illusion. When you learn or undo your particular lesson by seeing it in a different way, there is a collapse of time. This is what the miracle of release is. Now you can go on to the next lesson until you run out of lessons to undo. When this is done, reincarnation is no more. You stand at the end of time, at the border of eternity. Here, your miracle is needed no more.

Paranormal – Any experience that is beyond the explanation of the five senses.

Passerby – A passerby is one in the process of withdrawing all attachments from the beliefs and investments that the world seems to offer. The passerby is aware that their experience of an ever-changing world is not home.[251] Keep moving.

Placebo Effect – The mistaken belief that some form outside of you was the reason for your healing. It may have been the need of the moment, but never the reason for your experience of release. Placebo effect is an example of mind over matter. Because you are afraid of your thoughts you need a source seemingly outside of your mind to heal it.

Recollection – The memory of a past body experience. The phrase *past life* is misleading. You only have One Life, and that you share as One Mind.

Reincarnation – The mind's dream of sequential body experiences.

Spiritual Guides – Spiritual guides symbolize any form outside of you that you believe holds answers you don't have. Somehow they seem to hold

---

[251] "Be passersby." The Gospel of Thomas #42.

wisdom's you don't possess. You perceive a need for spiritual guides as long as you think you are separate from your Source of Wisdom.

Symbols of Power – Beliefs are your Symbols of Power. Every belief you assign value to in the forms the world presents is your investment. Your investments are where your treasures lie. Your mind becomes sick or is in a dream state when you limit it to transitory investments. The changing of your mind about any particular belief is your miracle, your undoing, your speed-up to peace of mind.

The Veil – The veil is that place *in-between* your body sense ephemeral experience and your ethereal / astral experience. The other side of the veil is not death but the continuation of your dream life in another form. When guilt catches up with you (karma), you are born again (reincarnate) to a body self-image.

Waking from the Dream – The process of real forgiveness being generalized to everything in the ephemeral. This process is about your journey to remember Source through your ephemeral experience. Waking up to what you already are is not about evolving. Nor is it about experiencing the astral realm. It is about waking up to what you already are.

Wanderer – In the world of appearances not everyone who wanders is lost. However, those who are lost to the world of symbols, wander the world seeking to invest in the experience of the illusion through the symbols of the ephemeral.

In a moment of great physical pain, a voice spoke to me in the night saying clearly ... "dying is as easy as letting go of the breath." And then the pain was gone.

Rita Karayan
February 2023

Made in the USA
Las Vegas, NV
09 February 2025